CW00954453

BUTTERFLIES IN COLOUR

BUTTERFLIES
in Colour

LEIF LYNEBORG

Illustrations by Werner Hancke

English edition
Translated by K. Campbell Ferguson
Edited by J. H. Midwinter

BLANDFORD PRESS
LONDON

Originally published in Denmark by Politikens Forlag 1974
First published in England 1974
by Blandford Press Ltd,
167 High Holborn, London WC1V 6PH
World Copyright © 1974
Politikens Forlag A/S
Copenhagen

ISBN 0 7137 0718 6

Printed in Great Britain by
Richard Clay (The Chaucer Press), Ltd.,
Bungay, Suffolk

Contents

Contents

PREFACE

Planned and written by Leif Lyneborg MA, in association with the artist Niels Jønsson, this volume covers Scandinavia and Europe west of a line from southern Sweden to the Adriatic.

In the first forty-four of the forty-eight colour plates more than two hundred species are shown, which represent approximately 75 per cent of all butterflies found in the area. The species which have been omitted either have limited areas of distribution or are difficult for the amateur to distinguish from other species. All species are shown on the colour plates in the scale 2:3, except nos. 6–9, which for reasons of space are shown to a smaller scale.

Besides a short introduction, the text comprises detailed descriptions of the species shown on the colour plates, supplemented by short introductions to the six families dealt with in this book.

The description of each species begins with a summary of the salient characteristics by which the species can be identified. Where the sexes differ, the male characteristics are described first, followed by the distinguishing characteristics of the female.

The 'Distribution' section deals principally with the range of the various species within the immediate scope of this book and also summarises the overall distribution.

The 'Habitat' section describes the habitats of the species giving specific altitudes.

The final section gives details of life history.

INTRODUCTION

Classification
Butterflies and moths (Lepidoptera) comprise one of the four large insect orders. The other orders are beetles (Coleoptera), bees and wasps (Hymenoptera) and flies (Diptera). The order Lepidoptera is subdivided into families, only six of which are described in this book, namely Papilionidae (swallowtails), Pieridae (whites), Libytheidae, Nymphalidae (browns), Lycaenidae (blues) and Hesperiidae (skippers).

Definition
'Butterflies' and 'moths' are terms of convenience and common usage rather than strict zoological names. Butterflies in Britain are diurnal and most moths nocturnal, but many moths are also diurnal and in the tropics there are nocturnal butterflies. However, there are anatomical differences, the most obvious of which are the antennae. Butterflies' antennae are always enlarged at the tip, whereas the antennae of moths taper evenly, or are shaped in some other way. Butterflies also lack the linkage between forewings and hind wings which distinguishes moths. Consequently butterflies usually rest with their wings folded vertically over their backs, whereas moths fold their wings horizontally.

Anatomy
The body of a butterfly may be divided into head, thorax and abdomen. The head bears a pair of large compound faceted eyes and a pair of long, many-jointed antennae. The antennae serve both sensory and olfactory functions. They enable the sexes to find each other, and enable the female to find the appropriate host plant on which to lay eggs. The proboscis is also borne on the head, coiled up under the head when not in use and uncoiled for sipping nectar or sap. Superficially a simple tube, the proboscis actually consists of several mouth parts, including a

pair of large, hairy triadic appendages, or palps, equipped with sense organs, and situated at the root of the proboscis. The colour of the antennae and palps can, occasionally, help to distinguish closely-related species of butterflies.

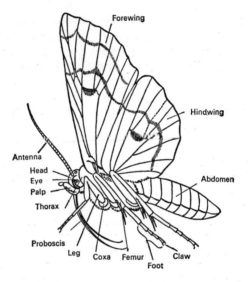

The thorax of a butterfly consists of three segments, each of which carries a pair of legs, while the second and third thoracic segments also support a pair of wings. The legs are divided into several parts, connected by joints. The two largest of the leg are the femur (thigh) and the tibia. At the base of the femur is a small trochanter. This forms a link to the coxa (hip), which is rigidly connected to the underside of the thorax. At the tip of the tibia is a many jointed foot, which bears claws at its tip. The front pair of legs of Nymphalid and some Lycaenid butterflies are reduced, lack claws and are no longer used for walking.

The wings of most butterflies are relatively large, and the forewings are not linked with the hind wings. They are covered with scales above and below. Each scale is a small plate attached to the wing surface by a short stalk. The scales are in rows and partly cover one another. The colours of a butterfly's wing may be produced by the different colours of the scales or by interference phenomena caused by the structure of the scales.

In addition to the usual scales, male butterflies also have scent scales (androconia), evenly distributed among the other scales or concentrated in stripes or spots which are in many cases dark. The roots of the scent scales are attached to the scent producing glands. The scent which evaporates from the scent scales is peculiar to each species and thus helps the two sexes to find each other.

A butterfly wing can generally be described as a rounded triangle. Its anterior side is termed the 'front edge' or costa (or just 'the edge'); its lateral edge 'the border'; and its posterior 'the back edge'. The wings are shaped to form an anterior and a posterior corner.

The area of the wing is divided into four 'sections': the root or basal section innermost; next is the discal section; then the post-discal section; and finally the sub-marginal section. Veins traverse the wing, as illustrated. These define 'cells', regions

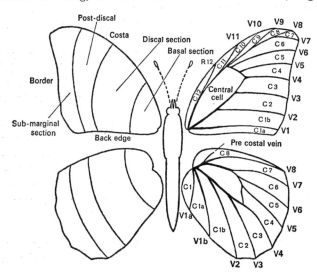

bounded by veins. Innermost is a large cell enclosed by major veins. This, the 'central cell', is the focus from which most other veins radiate.

Veins are indicated numerically on the diagram; vein no. 1 lies at the posterior edge of the wing. It is usually most convenient to start counting from vein no. 2, which arises near the middle of the posterior edge of the central cell. Counting forward from vein no. 2 there are usually ten more veins (veins nos. 3–12) on the forewings. Together with vein no. 1, seen just inside the back edge, these comprise twelve veins. There are exceptions, vein no. 1 of the anterior wings in swallowtails (Papilionidae) is divided making a total of thirteen veins. Certain Lycaenid species have only ten or eleven veins, owing to the disappearance of certain veins. Hind wings bear six veins (veins nos. 3–8) anterior to vein no. 2; vein no. 1 is divided in all species except swallowtails. Consequently, the hind wings of swallowtails bear only eight whereas those of other butterflies bear nine. On the hind wing there is usually a separate, minor precostal vein along the front edge near the attachment.

The cells of a butterfly wing (not to be confused with the 'sections' mentioned earlier), are numbered, so that cell no. 2 lies anterior to vein no. 2 and so on.

The abdomen consists of eleven segments, only seven being visible. The external sex organs are located at the tip of the abdomen. The anatomy of the sex organs (genitalia), especially of males, is important for classification, and many species can only be distinguished by a study of these.

It can be difficult to determine the sex of a butterfly. Normally, the abdomen of the female is broad and blunt posteriorly; careful examination with a magnifying glass or microscope may reveal the tip of the ovipositor as a pair of hairy lobes. The abdomen of the male is usually slim and bears pincers (valves) terminally. Between them the tip of the genitalia can sometimes be seen.

Distribution
Europe is part of the palaearctic faunal region. This region also includes North Africa south to the Sahara, as well as the tem-

perate zones of Asia, including Japan. The butterfly fauna of Europe is comparatively unlike the tropics.

The European continent has undergone great changes within the last million years; namely, several glacial periods with intervening warmer periods, radical changes in the vegetation in relation to the geophysical conditions, and within the last couple of thousand years the fundamental changes in flora and fauna wrought by man. These changes are reflected in the present distribution of butterflies as of other animals.

As a general rule, the presence of a particular butterfly species indicates that the prevailing climate and vegetation conditions of that area are suitable for it. However, the species may not occur wherever the right conditions prevail: physical barriers may prevent the spread of a species, or the habitat may be occupied by another species.

Many butterfly species of Europe are limited to mountains, especially the Alps and the Pyrenees, but many are also found in other southern and central European mountains. Another considerable number of species are southern European, found in Spain, Portugal, southern France, Italy and in the Balkans, as well as North Africa. There is also a large group of southern and central European species which are not found north of a line running from central Germany to southern Scandinavia. These species usually do not occur near the North Sea or in the British Isles.

Other species are found further north, and reach their northern limit in central Sweden and southern Finland; these species are occasionally found in parts of Britain. The fauna of Scandinavia and Finland includes certain northern species which are not found elsewhere in Europe, with the exception, perhaps, of some central European mountains. Finally, there are some widely distributed species which can be found throughout Europe. These species often prove to be circumpolar in distribution, that is, they are also found in North America. It is common to many species that they are not found near the Atlantic or North Sea coasts of European countries. Such continental species do not thrive in the colder climate, the wind, and the greater precipitation of the coastal region.

Nomenclature

By 1758 many of the most common butterflies had been named by the Swedish naturalist, Carl von Linne (Linnaeus 1707–78), the founder of biological nomenclature. According to his system, every organism is identified by a Latin generic name, followed by a specific name and, occasionally, also by a subspecific name. Neither specific nor subspecific name is capitalised but the whole Latin name is italicised. Thus, the speckled wood butterfly (no. 133) was named *Satyrus aegeria* by Linnaeus and the description made in 1758 was based on species found in southern Europe and North Africa.

Early scientists like Linnaeus only worked with a few large butterfly genera, among them *Satyrus*. During the following centuries these large heterogenous genera were frequently subdivided. One of these, the genus *Pararge*, was created in 1818 by the German Hübner and comprised the *aegeria* of Linnaeus and a number of closely related species. The name used today to specify the speckled wood butterfly is *Pararge aegeria*. It was later found that the speckled wood butterfly of central and northern Europe is lighter than the species found in southern Europe which Linnaeus had seen and described. In 1867, Butler, on the basis of French specimens, named these lighter speckled wood butterflies *Pararge tircis*. However, the two butterflies described by Linnaeus and Butler were merely different subspecies of the same species. The butterfly described earliest is therefore named *Pararge aegeria aegeria*, whereas the butterfly named later is called *Pararge aegeria tircis*. Briefly, subspecies are separated geographically, but can crossbreed and produce a fertile brood; but different species cannot crossbreed.

It is, however, never easy to decide whether slightly differing butterfly populations are actually different species or only subspecies. It must be remembered that species are constantly evolving and their characteristics may be unstable. Among European butterflies there are certain species whose characteristics change gradually from one area to another. The extreme variations of such a 'cline' can easily be distinguished from each other, but it is impossible to draw any sharp distinction anywhere along the cline; in other words, the species cannot be divided into geographically distinct subspecies. Clines often indicate evolution of subspecies and a subspecies will evolve if certain populations are isolated by physical barriers.

Many scientists have named populations of local occurrence, or populations which differed only slightly. These could, for instance, be populations on a certain mountainous area, or in an isolated valley, but these have been omitted.

Some butterflies show seasonal variations, that is, the summer generation differs from the spring generation. A good example is the map butterfly, *Araschnia levana* (no. 51). 'Form' names often describe seasonal variants, but such names must not be confused with the subspecific names.

Life History

Butterflies undergo a complete metamorphosis, that is, the individual which hatches from the egg is strikingly different from the adult butterfly. The egg, larva and pupa are the development stages of the butterfly.

Butterflies' tiny eggs have many different shapes. Some are barrel- or bottle-shaped, others conical or hemispherical, and others are flat. They also vary in colour and often change colour during development. Many butterfly eggs are ribbed or covered with a network of thickenings.

Usually the female butterfly places her eggs on or near the food plant of the larva. Sometimes many eggs are placed together, forming a 'cake', at other times the eggs are placed singly. Eggs usually hatch into larvae within a fortnight, but some over-winter.

The larvae of the various butterfly species vary considerably and some of their salient characteristics are described in the introduction to families in the section following the colour plates.

The butterfly larva consists of thirteen segments plus the head. The first three are thoracic segments, each of which has one pair of true, jointed gressorial (walking) legs. The next ten are abdominal segments, but the two last segments are not always divided. On the third to sixth abdominal segments pairs of prolegs are found; these are false, inarticulate limbs equipped with hooks. There is also a pair of prolegs, or claspers, on the last abdominal segment. The larva has biting mouth parts, which are of a completely different structure from those of the adult butterfly. Spinning glands are situated in the head. The threads are employed by the larva in various ways, as for tying leaves together, for fastening the larva to vegetation, and for spinning a cocoon.

When the tiny larva has hatched it often eats the egg shell and then proceeds to eat vegetation. The larva has to cast its skin several times to enable it to grow, since the exoskeleton stretches scarcely at all and thus limits growth. During moulting a new exoskeleton is created inside the old one, which then bursts, and the larva crawls out. The number of moults varies among species. The larval stages of the same species may also differ somewhat.

The larval stage may last a fortnight to two years. When species have two generations each season the larvae of the spring grow up quickly, whereas the larvae of the summer generation often overwinter and eat both before and after hibernation.

The pupa embodies the last of the immature stages and bears more resemblance to the butterfly: for instance, wings and legs are visible. The organs of the larva disintegrate inside the pupa while the organs of the adult butterfly form. Butterfly pupae usually hang very freely, often suspended by a couple of hooks at the posterior. Some, such as the garden white pupae, are also supported by a girdle of silk round their middle. Other pupae lie freely on the ground without any protective cocoon, while 'skipper' pupae are suspended in a loosely-spun cocoon.

The length of the pupal stage varies considerably. Species which overwinter as larvae usually have a pupal stage of two to three weeks. Other species which pupate in the autumn may or may not emerge as butterflies before spring.

1. *Parnassius apollo*, Apollo, male.—2. *Parnassius phoebus sacerdos*, Small Apollo, male.—3. *Parnassius mnemosyne mnemosyne*, Clouded Apollo, male.—4. *Zerynthia rumina*, Spanish Festoon, male.—5. *Zerynthia polyxena*, Southern Festoon, female.

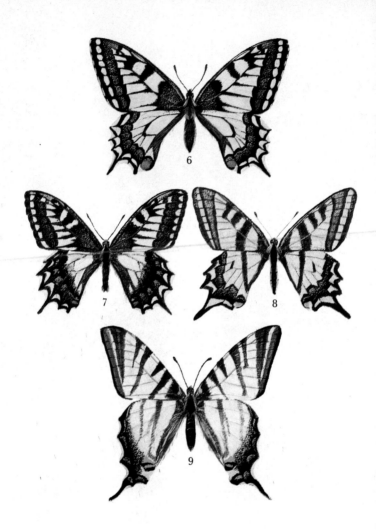

6. *Papilio machaon*, Swallowtail, male.—7. *Papilio hospiton*, Corsican Swallowtail, male.—8. *Papilio alexanor*, Southern Swallowtail, male.—9. *Iphiclides
podalirius podalirius*, Scarce Swallowtail, male of first generation.

10. *Aporia crataegi*, Black-veined White, male; a. female.—11. *Pieris brassicae*, Large White, male; a. female.—12. *Pieris rapae*, Small White, male; a. female.—13. *Pieris mannii*, Southern Small White, male.—14. *Pieris ergane*, Mountain Small White, male.

15. *Pieris napi napi*, Green-veined White, male of first generation; a. female. —16. *Pontia daplidice*, Bath White, male; a. underside; b. female.—17. *Pontia callidice*, Peak White, male.—18. *Euchloe ausonia crameri*, Dappled White, male; a. underside. — 19. *Euchloe belemia*, Green-striped White, male.

20. *Anthocharis belia euphenoides*, Morocco Orange Tip, male; a. female.—21.
Anthocharis cardamines, Orange Tip, male; a. female.—22. *Zegris eupheme*,
Sooty Orange Tip, male.—23. *Colias phicomone*, Mountain Clouded Yellow,
male; a. female.—24. *Colias nastes werdandi*, Pale Arctic Clouded Yellow,
male.

25. *Colias palaeno*, Moorland Clouded Yellow, male; a. female.—26. *Colias crocea*, Clouded Yellow, male; a. female.—27. *Colias myrmidone*, Danube Clouded Yellow, male; a. female.—28. *Colias hecla sulitelma*, Northern Clouded Yellow, male; a. female.

29. *Colias hyale*, Pale Clouded Yellow, male; a. female.—30. *Gonepteryx rhamni*, Brimstone, male; a. female.—31. *Gonepteryx cleopatra*, Cleopatra, male.—32. *Leptidea sinapis*, Wood White, male; a. female.

33. *Libythea celtis*, Nettle-tree Butterfly, male.—34. *Apatura iris*, Purple Emperor, male; a. female.—35. *Apatura ilia*, Small Purple Emperor, male. —36. *Neptis rivularis*, Hungarian Glider, male.

37. *Charaxes jasius*, Two-tailed Pasha, male; a. underside.—38. *Limenitis populi*, Poplar Admiral, male; a. underside.

39. *Limenitis camilla*, White Admiral, male; a. underside.—40. *Limenitis reducta*, Southern White Admiral, male; a. underside.—41. *Nymphalis antiopa*, Camberwell Beauty, male.

42. *Nymphalis polychloros*, Large Tortoiseshell, male.—43. *Nymphalis xantho-melas*, Yellow-legged Tortoiseshell, male.—44. *Inachis io*, Peacock, male.—45. *Polygonia c-album*, Comma, male; a. underside.

46. *Vanessa atalanta*, Red Admiral, male.—47. *Vanessa cardui*, Painted Lady, male; a. underside.—48. *Aglais urticae*, Small Tortoiseshell, male.—49. *Argynnis paphia*, Silver-washed Fritillary, male; a. underside.

50. *Pandoriana pandora*, Cardinal, female; a. underside.—51. *Araschnia levana*, Map Butterfly, male of 1st generation; a. male of 2nd generation.

52. *Mesoacidalia aglaja*, Dark Green Fritillary, male; a. underside. 53.
Fabriciana adippe, High Brown Fritillary, male; a. underside. — 54. *Fabriciana niobe*, Niobe Fritillary, male; a. underside. — 55. *Issoria lathonia*, Queen of Spain Fritillary, male; a. underside.

56. *Brenthis hecate*, Twin-spot Fritillary, male; a. underside.—57. *Brenthis daphne*, Marbled Fritillary, male; a. underside.—58. *Brenthis ino*, Lesser Marbled Fritillary, male; a. underside.—59. *Boloria napaea*, Mountain Fritillary, female; a. male, underside.

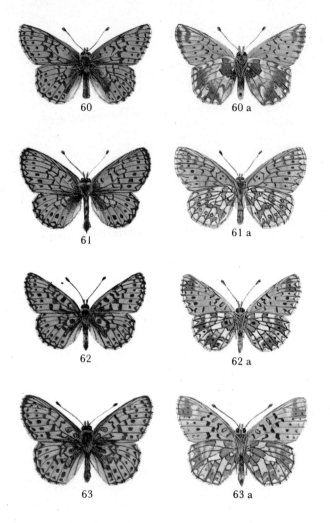

60. *Boloria aquilonaris*, Cranberry Fritillary, male; a. underside.—61. *Proclossiana eunomia*, Bog Fritillary, male; a. female, underside. 62. *Clossiana selene*, Small Pearl-bordered Fritillary, male; a. underside.—63. *Clossiana euphrosyne*, Pearl-bordered Fritillary, male; a. underside.

64. *Clossiana titania cypris*, Titania's Fritillary, male; a. underside.—65. *Clossiana freija*, Frejya's Fritillary, female; a. male, underside.—66. *Clossiana chariclea*, Arctic Fritillary, female, underside.—67. *Clossiana improba*, Dusky-winged Fritillary, male.—68. *Clossiana dia*, Violet Fritillary, male; a. underside.—69. *Clossiana thore*, Thor's Fritillary, male; a. underside.

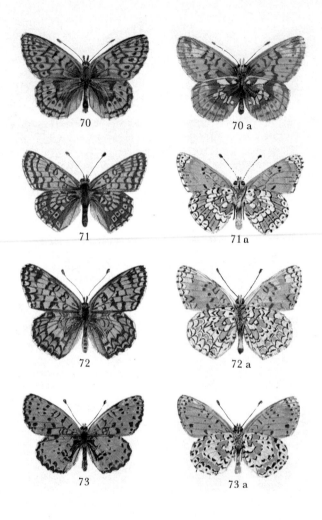

70. *Clossiana frigga*, Frigg's Fritillary, male; a. underside.—71. *Melitaea cinxia*, Glanville Fritillary, male; a. underside.—72. *Melitaea phoebe phoebe*, Knapweed Fritillary, male; a. underside.—73. *Melitaea didyma meridionalis*, Spotted Fritillary, male; a. underside.

74. *Melitaea diamina*, False Heath Fritillary, male; a. underside.—75. *Mellicta athalia athalia*, Heath Fritillary, female; a. male, underside.—76. *Mellicta deione deione*, Provencal Fritillary, male; a. underside.—77 *Mellicta parthenoides*, Meadow Fritillary, male.—78. *Mellicta aurelia*, Nickerl's Fritillary, male; a. underside.

79. *Euphydryas maturna*, Scarce Fritillary, male; a. underside.—80. *Euphydryas iduna*, Lapland Fritillary, male.—81. *Euphydryas cynthia*, Cynthia's Fritillary, male; a. underside; b. female.—82. *Euphydryas aurinia aurinia*, Marsh Fritillary, male; a. underside.

83. *Melanargia galathea*, Marbled White, male; a. underside.—84. *Melanargia russiae*, Esper's Marbled White, male; a. underside.—85. *Melanargia occitanica*, Western Marbled White, male; a. underside.

86. *Melanargia arge*, Italian Marbled White, male; a. underside.—87. *Melanargia ines*, Spanish Marbled White, male; a. underside.—88. *Hipparchia fagi*, Woodland Grayling, female.

89. *Hipparchia alcyone*, Rock Grayling, female.—90. *Hipparchia neomiris*, Corsican Grayling, male.—91. *Hipparchia semele*, Grayling, male; a. underside; b. female.—92. *Hipparchia aristaeus*, Southern Grayling, female.

93. *Hipparchia statilinus*, Tree Grayling, male; a. underside.—94. *Pseudo-tergumia fidia*, Striped Grayling, male, underside.—95. *Chazara briseis*, Hermit, male; a. underside.

96. *Oeneis bore*, Arctic Grayling, male.—97. *Oeneis norna*, Norse Grayling, male; a. underside.—98. *Oeneis glacialis*, Alpine Grayling, male; a. underside.—99. *Oeneis jutta*, Baltic Grayling, male; a. female.

100. *Satyrus actaea*, Black Satyr, male; a. underside.—101. *Satyrus ferula*, Sooty Satyr, male; a. underside; b. female.—102. *Minois dryas*, Dryad, male.

103. *Arethusana arethusa*, False Grayling, male; a. female.—104. *Brintesia circe*, Banded Grayling, male.—105. *Erebia embla*, Lapland Ringlet, female. 106. *Erebia disa*, Arctic Ringlet, female.—107. *Erebia pandrosa*, Dewy Ringlet, male; a. underside.

108. *Erebia medusa*, Woodland Ringlet, male; a. underside.—109. *Erebia ligea*, Arran Brown, male, a. underside.—10. *Erebia euryale*, Large Ringlet, male.—111. *Erebia aethiops*, Scotch Argus, male; a. underside.—112. *Erebia epistygne*, Spring Ringlet, male.

113. *Erebia epiphron*, Mountain Ringlet, male; a. female, underside.—114.
Erebia pharte, Blind Ringlet, male; a. female, underside.—115. *Erebia gorge
gorge*, Silky Ringlet, male; a. subspecies *ramondi*, female.—116. *Erebia
cassioides*, Brassy Ringlet, male.—117. *Erebia neoridas*, Autumn Ringlet,
male.

118. *Erebia pronoe*, Water Ringlet, male; a. underside.—119. *Erebia oeme*, Bright-eyed Ringlet, male; a. female, underside.—120. *Maniola jurtina*, Meadow Brown, male; a. female.—121. *Hyponephele lycaon*, Dusky Meadow Brown, male; a. female, underside.

122. *Aphantopus hyperantus*, Ringlet, male; a. underside.—123. *Pyronia tithonus*, Gatekeeper, male; a. underside; b. female.—124. *Pyronia cecilia*, Southern Gatekeeper, male; a. underside; b. female.

125. *Pyronia bathseba*, Spanish Gatekeeper, male; a. underside; b. female.—
126. *Coenonympha tullia*, Large Heath, male; a. underside; b. female.—127.
Coenonympha pamphilus, Small Heath, male; a. underside.—128. *Coenonympha dorus*, Dusky Heath, male; a. underside.—129. *Coenonympha arcania*, Pearly Heath, male; a. underside.

130. *Coenonympha hero*, Scarce Heath, male; a. underside. — 131. *Coenonympha glycerion*, Chestnut Heath, male; a. underside. — 132. *Coenonympha oedippus*, False Ringlet, male; a. underside. — 133. *Pararge aegeria aegeria*, Speckled Wood, male from Italy; a. subspecies *tircis* from Denmark. — 134. *Lasiommata megera*, Wall Brown, male; a. female.

135. *Lasiommata maera maera*, Large Wall Brown, male; a. female; b. male of subspecies *adrasta* from Italy; c. female of same.—136. *Lasiommata petro-politana*, Northern Wall Brown, male; a. female.—137. *Lopinga achine*, Woodland Brown, male.

138. *Hamearis lucina*, Duke of Burgundy Fritillary, male; a. underside. — 139. *Thecla betulae*, Brown Hairstreak, male; a. underside; b. female. — 140. *Quercusia quercus*, Purple Hairstreak, male; a. underside; b. female. — 141. *Laeosopis roboris*, Spanish Purple Hairstreak, male; a. underside. — 142. *Nordmannia acaciae*, Sloe Hairstreak, male; a. underside. — 143. *Nordmannia esculi*, False Ilex Hairstreak, male; a. underside.

144. *Nordmannia ilicus*, Ilex Hairstreak, male; a. underside; b. female.—
145. *Strymonidia spini*, Blue-spot Hairstreak, male, underside.—146. *Strymonidia w-album*, White-letter Hairstreak, male; a. underside.—147. *Strymonidia pruni*, Black Hairstreak, male; a. underside.—148. *Callophrys rubi*, Green Hairstreak, female; a. underside.—149. *Tomares ballus*, Provence Hairstreak, male; a. underside; b. female.

150. *Lycaena helle*, Violet Copper, male; a. underside; b. female. — 151. *Lycaena phlaeas*, Small Copper, male; a. underside. — 152. *Lycaena dispar*, Large Copper, male; a. underside; b. female. — 153. *Heodes tityrus*, Sooty Copper, male; a. female. — 154. *Heodes virgaureae*, Scarce Copper, male; a. underside; b. female.

155. *Heodes alciphron alciphron*, Purple-shot Copper, male; a. female. — 156. *Heodes alciphron gordius*, Swiss Purple-shot Copper, male; a. female. — 157. *Thersamonia thersamon*, Lesser Fiery Copper, male. — 158. *Palaeochrysophanus hippothoe hippothoe*, Purple-edged Copper, male; a. female. — 159. *Palaeochryso-phanus hippothoe eurydame*, male. — 160. *Lampides boeticus*, Long-tailed Blue, male; a. underside; b. female. — 161. *Syntarucus pirithous*, Lang's Short-tailed Blue, male; a. underside; b. female.

162. *Everes argiades*, Short-tailed Blue, male; a. underside.— 163. *Cupido osiris*, Osiris Blue, male.— 164. *Cupido minimus*, Small Blue, male; a. under-side.— 165. *Celastrina argiolus*, Holly Blue, male; a. underside; b. female.— 166. *Glaucopsyche alexis*, Green-underside Blue, male; a. underside.— 167. *Maculinea alcon alcon*, Alcon Blue, male; a. underside; b. female.

168. *Maculinea arion*, Large Blue, male; a. underside.—169. *Maculinea teleius*, Scarce Large Blue, male; a. underside.—170. *Maculinea nausithous*, Dusky Large Blue, male; a. underside.—171. *Iolana iolas*, Iolas Blue, male; a. female.—172. *Philotes baton*, Baton Blue, male; a. underside.—173. *Scoliantides orion*, Chequered Blue, male; a. underside.—174. *Plebeius argus*, Silver-studded Blue, male; a. female.

175. *Lycaeides idas*, Idas Blue, male; a. female.—176. *Vacciniina optilete*, Cranberry Blue, male; a. underside.—177. *Eumedonia eumedon*, Geranium Argus, male; a. underside.—178. *Aricia agestis*, Brown Argus, male; a. underside.—179. *Aricia agestis artaxerxes*, Scotch Argus, male.—180. *Aricia artaxerxes inhonora*, male; a. underside.—181. *Aricia cramera*, Southern Brown Argus, male.—182. *Aricia nicias*, Silvery Argus, male; a. underside.—183. *Albulina orbitulus*, Alpine Argus, male; a. underside.—184. *Cyaniris semiargus*, Mazarine Blue, male; a. underside.

185. *Agrodiaetus damon.* Damon Blue, male; a. underside. — 186. *Agrodiaetus ripartii*, Ripart's Blue, male. — 187. *Plebicula escheri escheri*, Escher's Blue, male; a. female. — 188. *Plebicula dorylas*, Turquoise Blue, male; a. underside. — 189. *Plebicula amanda*, Amanda's Blue, male; a. underside; b. female. — 190. *Meleageria daphnis*, Meleager's Blue, male; a. female. — 191. *Lysandra coridon*, Chalk-hill Blue, male; a. female.

192. *Lysandra albicans*, Spanish Chalk-hill Blue, male.—193. *Lysandra bellargus*, Adonis Blue, male; a. underside. — 194. *Polyommatus icarus*, Common Blue, male; a. underside; b. female. — 195. *Pyrgus malvae*, Grizzled Skipper, male.—196. *Pyrgus alveus*, Large Grizzled Skipper, male; a. underside.— 197. *Pyrgus armoricanus*, Oberthur's Grizzled Skipper, male.—198. *Pyrgus serratulae*, Olive Skipper, male, underside.—199. *Pyrgus centaureae*, Northern Grizzled Skipper, male, underside.—200. *Pyrgus fritillarius*, Safflower Skipper, male; a. underside.—201. *Muschampia proto*, Large Grizzled Skipper, male.

202. *Spialia sertorius*, Red-underwing Skipper, male; a. underside.—203. *Carcharodus alceae*, Mallow Skipper, male.—204. *Carcharodus lavatherae*, Marbled Skipper, male.—205. *Carcharodus boeticus*, Southern Marbled Skipper, male.—206. *Carcharodus flocciferus*, Tufted Skipper, male; a. underside.—207. *Erynnis tages*, Dingy Skipper, male.—208. *Herteropterus morpheus*, Large Chequered Skipper, male; a. underside.—209. *Cartero-cephalus palaemon*, Chequered Skipper, male.—210. *Carterocephalus silvicolus*, Northern Chequered Skipper, male.—211. *Thymelicus acteon*, Lulworth

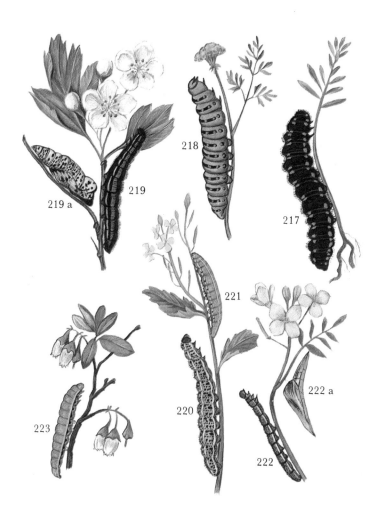

Skipper, male; a. female.—212. *Thymelicus lineola*, Essex Skipper, male.—
213. *Thymelicus sylvestris*, Small Skipper, male.—214. *Ochlodes venatus*, Large
Skipper, male.—215. *Hesperia comma*, Silver-spotted Skipper; a. underside.
—216. *Gegenes nostradamus*, Mediterranean Skipper, male.
217. *Parnassius apollo*, Apollo.—218. *Papilio machaon*, Swallowtail.—219.
Aporia crataegi, Black-veined White; a. pupa.—220. *Pieris brassicae*, Large
White.—221. *Pieris rapae*, Small White.—222. *Anthocharis cardamines*, Orange
Tip; a. pupa.—223. *Colias palaeno*, Moorland Clouded Yellow.

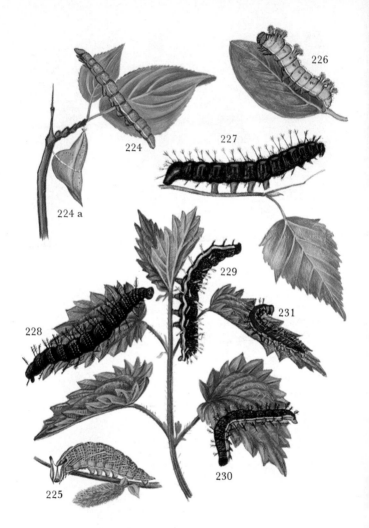

224. *Gonepteryx rhamni*, Brimstone; a. pupa.—225. *Apatura iris*, Purple Emperor.—226. *Limenitis camilla*, White Admiral.—227. *Nymphalis antiopa*, Camberwell Beauty.—228. *Inachis io*, Peacock.—229. *Vanessa atalanta*, Red Admiral.—230. *Aglais urticae*, Small Tortoiseshell.—231. *Araschnia levana*, Map Butterfly.

232. *Argynnis paphia*, Silver-washed Fritillary. — 233. *Mesoacidalia aglaja*, Dark-green Fritillary. — 234. *Fabriciana niobe*, Niobe Fritillary. — 235. *Brenthis ino*, Lesser Marbled Fritillary. — 236. *Mellicta athalia*, Heath Fritillary. — 237. *Euphydryas maturna*, Scarce Fritillary. — 238. *Melanargia galathea*, Marbled White. — 239. *Hipparchia semele*, Grayling.

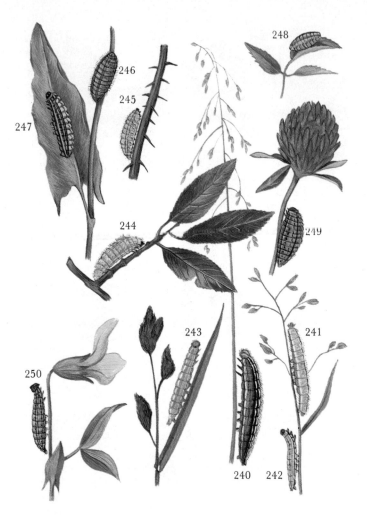

240. *Erebia medusa*, Woodland Ringlet.—241. *Maniola jurtina*, Meadow Brown.—242. *Coenonympha pamphilus*, Small Heath.—243. *Lasiommata megera*, Wall Brown.—244. *Thecla betulae*, Brown Hairstreak.—245. *Callophrys rubi*, Green Hairstreak.—246. *Lycaena phlaeas*, Small Copper.—247. *Heodes virgaureae*, Scarce Copper.—248. *Cupido minimus*, Small Blue.—249. *Lysandra bellargus*, Adonis Blue.—250. *Erynnis tages*, Dingy Skipper.

DESCRIPTIONS OF THE BUTTERFLIES

PAPILIONIDAE (SWALLOWTAILS)

The Papilionidae, or swallowtails, are a fairly small butterfly family, comprising about six hundred species. However, as there are numerous subspecies, seasonal and individual variations, the existing scientific names number several thousand. The family is found all over the world, but especially in warmer regions, and the greatest number of species is found in the Indo-Australian region. Only about ten species are found in Europe, a couple of which are restricted to the Balkans.

The chief characteristic of the family is that all six legs of the adult butterfly develop in the same way, whereas the forelegs of the Nymphalidae are reduced. Each foot has a single pair of claws, while the antennae thicken evenly towards the end, unlike the more typical claviform antennae of other families. The larvae of all papilionid butterflies have a characteristic forked, brightly-coloured osmeterium situated just behind the head capsule. This is a defensive organ which can be extruded to give off a pungent secretion if the larva is disturbed.

1 *Parnassius apollo*
  Apollo
Characteristics: Male: Wing length 35–42 mm. On topside of forewing is a big, black spot in cell 1b, immediately in front of the back edge. Topside of hind wing has big, red ocelli, which are sometimes yellow. Female similar to male, but topside is often greyer and ocelli bigger. Red spots may also occur in post-discal section on forewing and in back corner of hind wings. Antennae have no clear rings (cf. the following species). Appearance of the species can vary considerably.
Distribution: Southern and central Sweden, southern Norway, southern Finland, as well as mountain areas of central and southern Europe; eastwards as far as central Asia. Not in British Isles or much of western and northern Europe. Several subspecies have been described, but all have fairly limited

distribution. Seven separate sub-species are known in Scandinavia and about 20 subspecies on the Iberian Peninsula.

Habitat: Mainly hilly and mountainous terrain, in central Europe up to 750–1,800 m in Scandinavia and southern Finland also in lowlands.

Life History: In Scandinavia on wing with its heavy, unsteady flight late June to mid-August, from May to September in Alps. Female has distinctive parchment-like sack under tip of abdomen; this congealed secretion is deposited by the male during mating, shortly after emergence from cocoon. Female deposits her eggs on stonecrop (*Sedum*) plants, where the extremely hardy eggs overwinter. For larva: see no. 217. Species protected in many countries.

2 *Parnassius phoebus sacerdos*
Alpine Apollo

Characteristics: Male: Wing length 30–33 mm. Usually noticeably smaller than Apollo (no. 1), with more yellowish-white ground colour. Near front edge of forewing (in cell 8) is post-discal spot usually with red centre. Spot in cell 1b near back edge of forewing (see plate) is small and black, if not absent altogether, while topside of hind wings has small ocelli. Female greyer, often with bigger red spots on hind wings, and usually black spot with red

centre in cell 1b on forewing. Antennae clearly ringed.

Distribution: Widespread in Asia and North America. In Europe subspecies *sacerdos* found in Alps, completely isolated from main areas of distribution.

Habitat: Mountains from 2,000 m upwards, often near streams and other damp habitats with grasses and other low plants.

Life History: On wing July–August. Larva similar to Apollo (no. 1), but smaller, slimmer, with more lemon or orange lateral spots. Lives on *Saxifraga aizioides* (yellow mountain saxifrage) and *Sempervivum montanum* (mountain houseleek).

3 *Parnassius mnemosyne mnemosyne*
Clouded Apollo

Characteristics: Male: Wing length 26–31 mm. White ground colour on topside. On forewing two black spots and broad grey band along edge. Hind wing has no red spots. Female similar, often with dark-grey dusting. Numerous subspecies, with considerable variation in size.

Distribution: Pyrenees and central France through central and southern Europe to Caucasus and central Asia; southern and central Scandinavia and Finland.

Habitat: Wooded lowlands in northern Europe in hilly or mountainous terrain to about 1,500 m in central and southern Europe.

Life History: On wing with its slow, heavy flight in sunny weather from early May to early August, depending on area; mainly in June in Scandinavia and Finland. Normally frequents very limited areas. visits flowers. White egg, shaped like sea urchin; probably overwinters. From April to May larva lives on various fumitory (*Corydalis*) species. Similar to Apollo larva, but with narrower extremities and more orange side spots. Pupa found in rather thick cocoon on ground, clay-yellow with white dusting.

4 *Zerynthia rumina*
Spanish Festoon
Characteristics: Male and female: Wing length 22–23 mm. Basic colour pale yellow, with numerous brownish-black bands and spots. Topside of forewing has big, red spots at base and top of central cell. Also small, red post-discal spots in cells 4, 5, 6 and 9; outside these, a hyaline spot. Sometimes a red spot shows near back edge of forewing (not illustrated). Hind wing has red spots along edge in cell 7 and red post-discal spots in cells 1–5. Considerable individual variation. European population divided into 5 subspecies, 4 in Spain and one in south-east France.
Distribution and Habitat: Spain, Portugal and south-east France. Also North Africa. Lives in uncultivated areas and on mountains from coast to 1,500 m.

Life History: On wing from late February to mid-May, especially on stony mountain sides near coast. Flies later at higher altitudes. One generation annually. Larva lives on various birthwort (*Aristolochia*) species.

5 *Zerynthia polyxena*
Southern Festoon
Characteristics: Male and female: Wing length 23–26 mm. Distinguished from no. 4 by absence of two red spots in central cell of forewing and absence of hyaline spot near wing tips. Moon pattern along border deeper than in *rumina* species (no. 4). May be red spot along edge of cell 9 of forewing (not shown in illustration). Extent of dark brown coloration varies.
Distribution: South-east France, where it accompanies *rumina* (no. 4), Italy, Sicily, and south-east Europe as far north as Austria and Moravia, provided situation is mild.
Habitat: Uncultivated stony places with sparse vegetation from coast to 1,000 m. Local occurrence.
Life History: On wing from late April to mid-May. Eggs deposited on underside of leaves of various birthwort (*Aristolochia*) species. Larva stays on plants for 4 weeks from May to July. Larva reddish-yellow or grey, with six rows of reddish-brown black-tipped tubercles. Once mature, larva has dark side stripe which stops short of last

segment. Pupa overwinters, occasionally only emerging after second winter.

6 *Papilio machaon*
Swallowtail

Characteristics: Male and female: Wing length 32–38 mm. Topside yellow and deep black, darker in the first generation than second. Broad black section at root of forewing. Submarginal band on underside of forewing enclosed by straight dark lines. Blue spots in post-discal band on hind wings paler in first generation, but more noticeable in second. Large red spot in corner of hind wings. Abdomen black in first generation, yellow with black back stripe in second. Considerable individual variation.

Distribution: Throughout Europe as far north as North Cape, but fairly rare in Scandinavia and Finland north of 64°N. Restricted to Cambridgeshire in British Isles. Also North Africa and throughout Asia to Japan. Closely-related species in North America.

Habitat: Breeds mainly in meadows and on hills with rich vegetation. Found up to 2,000 m in Alps. Likes open, dry and warm situations.

Life History: Two generations, the first from pupae which have over-wintered, on wing April–May, less numerous second generation, on wing July–August. In favourable years third generation may be on wing September–October. Swallowtail is strong, agile flier, and difficult to catch in flight. Lives about 4 weeks and congregates particularly in high places. Females deposit smooth, almost spherical eggs singly on food plants, notably on fennel (*Ferula communis*) in British Isles. Elsewhere carrot (*Daucus*) or other umbellifers serve as food plants. For larva: see no. 218.

7 *Papilio hospiton*
Corsican Swallowtail

Characteristics: Male and female: Wing length 36–38 mm. Distinguished from *machaon* (no. 6) by shorter tail on hind wing, smaller, more precise blue spots on hind wings, tiny red spots in corners of hind wings, and dark, wavy lines enclosing submarginal band on underside of forewing.

Distribution and Habitat: Corsica and Sardinia, mainly on mountain slopes with vegetation between 600–1,200 m.

Life History: One generation annually, on wing May–July. Larva found on umbellifers, especially fennel (*Ferula communis*) and *Ruta corsica*.

8 *Papilio alexanor*
Southern Swallowtail

Characteristics: Male: Wing length 31–33 mm. Easily distinguished from two previous Papilio species by broad yellow band at root of forewing. Female larger.

Distribution: South-east France (Provence), southern Italy and Sicily, and the Balkans. Also western Asia as far as Iran and Turkestan.

Habitat: Mountain sides to 1,200 m. Very local and rare. Concentrated in southern French departments of Var and Basses Alpes.

Life History: Single generation. It has an extremely fast and competent flight on wing from May to July. Like other European Papilio species, larva lives on umbellifers, such as *Trinia vulgaris*, mountain meadow seseli (*Seseli montanum*) and *Ptychatis heterophylla*.

9 *Iphiclides podalirius podalirius*
Scarce Swallowtail

Characteristics: Male: Wing length 32–40 mm, female often bigger. Topside pale yellow to cream-coloured, with 6 broad black bands on forewing. Long tail on hind wing; orange crescent on corner spot. Two small black discal bands on underside of hind wings. Area between bands orange on first generation which have black abdomens. Second generation have black abdomens with light grey tips.

Distribution: North Africa and Iberian Peninsula through France to central and southern Europe, and eastwards through temperate parts of Asia to China. Northern limit is Saxony and central Poland, but occasional species found further north in Europe. Spanish and Portuguese populations found on southern slopes of Pyrenees are treated as separate subspecies, *feisihamelii.*

Habitat: Central and southern European lowlands near orchards and hedges, but also up to about 1,600 m. In spring, butterflies often congregate in high places but spend summer in moist areas.

Life History: North of Alps only one generation on wing May–July. South of Alps two generations, on wing May–June and July–August. Eggs laid singly on underside of leaves of sloe (*Prunus*), cherry (*Cerasus*) and hawthorn (*Crataegus*). In southern Europe also use leaves of other *Prunus* species, such as peach and almond. Fully-grown larva 30–40 mm long, smooth, anteriorly enlarged, green with yellow back and side stripes, yellow diagonal stripes and brown spots. Hibernating pupa yellow or brown, expanded in middle. Sloe now protected in Germany in general attempt to boost butterfly population which has been dwindling for last twenty years.

PIERIDAE (GARDEN WHITES)

The widely distributed family Pieridae, or garden whites, includes about 1,500 species, mostly white or yellow, often with dark spots. The sexes are usually distinct, and the various generations are often distinct too. Larvae are usually green, with few hairs, feeding mainly on crucifers and plants of the pea family. The forelegs are not reduced like those of the Nymphalidae species, and the claws are characteristically forked; wing scales contain pigments of the pterin group (derivatives of uric acid).

10 *Aporia crataegi*
Black-veined White
Characteristics: Male: Wing length 28–34 mm. Topside of wings is basically white. Veins pronounced. Small black spot near outside edge of central cell on forewing. Underside similar to topside, but often darkened slightly by scattered black scales. Female (no. 10a) usually bigger and less transparent, with less 'dusting' on wings.
Distribution: Most parts of Europe, outside British Isles, Scandinavia and Finland, north of 62°N. Also North Africa and temperate zones of Asia to Japan.
Habitat: Open land with hedgerows and spinneys. In Alps to about 2,000 m. Characteristically unstable population wtih great fluctuation in numbers.
Life History: On wing with its heavy flight May–July. Visits clover and lucerne fields as well as wild flowers. Both butterfly and larva have unpleasant smell. Eggs deposited in groups of 100–200

on various trees of the families Pomaceae and Drupaceae, but particularly hawthorn (*Crataegus*). For larva: see no. 219.

11 *Pieris brassicae*
Large White
Characteristics: Male: Wing length 28–33 mm. Topside whitish, forewing has broad brownish-black rim as far as cell 3 or beyond. Hind wing has black spot near front edge. Black spots in cells 1b and 3 on underside of forewing. The female (no. 11a) often slightly bigger, with black spots in cells 1b and 3 on topside of forewing and black line along back edge. Topside of hind wing often yellower. Summer generation bigger than spring and autumn generations with broader black rim on wings. Temperature during development determines these differences.
Distribution: Throughout Europe, but seldom north of 62°N in Scandinavia and Finland. Also North Africa and Asia to Himalayas.

Habitat: Throughout British Isles. Spring population sometimes swelled by migration from south with subsequent increase in summer generation. Open places up to considerable altitude.

Life History: In western Europe first generation on wing May–June, second generation mid-July to mid-August. In hot summers partial third generation on wing in autumn. Females of spring generation deposit eggs on various wild crucifers, while females of summer generation oviposit on cultivated plants, such as swedes, cabbages, white mustard, rape and nasturtium (*Tropaeolum*). Eggs concentrated in single layer on both sides of leaves, often in groups of 40 to 100. Larvae may defoliate entire crops.

12 *Pieris rapae*
Small White

Characteristics: Male: Wing length 23–27 mm, usually noticeably smaller than no. 11. Dark grey spots on topside on first, darker on later generations. Dark rim on topside of forewing along wing tip to vein 6 or 7, also small dark spot in cell 3. Spots in cells 1b and 3 on underside of forewing. Female (no. 12a) has a greyish dusting at root of wings and diagonal spot in cell 1b.

Distribution: Throughout Europe but seldom north of about 62°N in Scandinavia and Finland. Most common butterfly in British Isles.

Also in North Africa and Asia to Japan.

Habitat: Cultivated land and up to 1,800 m in central Europe.

Life History: Two generations, occasionally three in British Isles and Denmark. Further south three or four generations normal, but only one generation further north. Species can migrate considerable distances. The 1 mm long, bottle-shaped eggs laid singly on undersides of leaves. For larva: see nos. 11, 221.

13 *Pieris mannii*
Southern Small White

Characteristics: Male: Wing length 20–23 mm. Very similar to small white (no. 12), but forewings relatively broader and shorter and 'border' more rounded. Spot at tip of forewing continues as narrow rim along 'border' as far as vein 3 or 4. Spot on front edge of hind wing concave on outside. Underside of hind wing covered by dark close-set scales. Female has broader band at tips, and spot in cell 3 usually clearly connected to border. Individuals of later generations often larger, darker and more widespread.

Distribution: France south of Loire, Italy, Sicily, eastern Spain and southern alpine valleys of Switzerland, Austria and Balkans. Also Morocco, Asia Minor and Syria.

Habitat and Life History: Favours cultivated land, like *rapae* (no. 12) but larva lives exclusively on wild crucifers. Three to four generations during summer. On wing from March until well into autumn.

14 *Pieris ergane*
Mountain Small White

Characteristics: Male: Wing length 19–24 mm. Very similar to small white (no. 12), but with squarer spot at tip of forewing, and no dark spots on underside of forewing; dark spot on topside in cell 3 may show through forewing; wing tip is yellowish. Topside of female's wings yellower, especially on hind wings, with bigger spot in cell 3 and faint spot in cell 1b.

Distribution: Europe confined to south-east France, Italian Apennines, some southern alpine valleys. Eastwards through Balkans to Asia Minor and Near East.

Habitat and Life History: Mainly grassy mountain slopes up to 1,800 m. Three generations on wing April to September, but much rarer in Europe than other whites. Larvae live on crucifers, especially *Aethionema saxatile*.

15 *Pieris napi napi*
Green-veined White

Characteristics: Male: Wing length 18–25 mm, larger in second generation. Occasional black spot in cell 3 on topside of forewing; wing tip spot has grey triangles at extreme ends of veins. Veins partly covered by grey dust. Underside of hind wings yellow with greenish dust along veins. Second generation males less grey along veins on topside of forewing and underside of hind wing. Females (no. 15a) darker with black spots in cells 1b and 3.

Distribution: Throughout Europe, but localised and rare in northern Scandinavia and Iberian Peninsula south of Madrid. Also North Africa, through Asia to Japan and North America.

Habitat: Throughout British Isles, with similar fluctuation in numbers to *Pieris brassicae* (no. 11). Open places, uncultivated and cultivated, up to 1,500 m.

Life History: Two or three generations annually, but only one at high altitudes. In British Isles, spring generation on wing May–June, summer generation July, autumn generation September. Eggs deposited singly on back of various wild crucifer leaves. Larva is fully grown and about 25 mm long in about 16 days. Dull green, with black, hairy tubercles on topside, and black spiracles surrounded by yellow ring. Colour of pupa varies. Cocoon is fixed to such things as poles and walls, or leaves of host plant.

Pieris napi bryoniae

A subspecies found in high Alps, Jura, and elsewhere. Similar to previous species, but greyer along veins; female particularly dark. Other very similar *napi* species found in Scandinavia and Finland.

16 *Pontia daplidice*
Bath White

Characteristics: Male: Wing length 21–24 mm. Dark wing tip spot on topside of forewing divided by white sections, and dark central spot divided by white line. Underside of forewing (no. 16a) has large central spot extending to front edge; greenish wing tip. Underside of hind wing spotted green. Female (no. 16b) similar to male, but more markings such as dark spot near back corner of forewing.

Distribution: Portugal, Spain and France through central and southern Europe. Occasional vagrants in England, Holland, north-west Germany and Jutland (Denmark). Indigenous to rest of Denmark and southern Sweden.

Habitat: Mainly uncultivated land with dry, sandy soil, but also fields and meadows with flowering clover (*Trifolium*), lucerne (*Medicago sativa*) and lupin (*Lupinus*).

Life History: In Scandinavia on wing May and July–September; in central Europe two or three generations on wing April–May, July–August, and September–October, respectively. Numbers fluctuate. Often seen on wing in southern Europe as early as February–March. Quick, irregular flight. Eggs deposited singly on leaves or flowers of crucifers or mignonette (*Reseda*). Fully-grown larva approximately 25 mm long, greyish-violet with two yellow side stripes. Pupa greenish, brownish or grey, with reddish tip to head. Rests suspended by thread in host plant for 2 weeks in summer, while pupa from summer generation overwinters.

17 *Pontia callidice*
Peak White

Characteristics: Male: Wing length 21–26 mm. Very similar to no. 16, but fainter markings on tip of forewing and smaller central spot without white line. Underside of hind wing usually yellow. Veins edged with grey-green stripes, which in post-discal section divide ground colour into arrowhead-shaped spots. Female darker on topside, with well-developed spots in post-discal section and along border. Underside similar to male.

Distribution: Pyrenees and Alps. Outside Europe through Asia Minor and Lebanon to Himalayas, Tibet and Mongolia. Closely-related species found in western mountain areas of North America.

Habitat: Grassy mountain slopes between 1,500 and 3,000 m.

Life History: Usually single generation in Alps, on wing late June to mid-July. In good years second generation on wing July–August. Larva lives on various crucifers, especially dwarf treacle mustard (*Erysimum pumilum*) and mignonette (*Reseda*). Very similar to *daplidice* larva (no. 16), but spotted yellow longitudinal stripes. Green or grey pupa often found under stones.

18 *Euchloe ausonia crameri*
Dappled White

Characteristics: Male: Wing length 20–24 mm. Topside of forewing tip greyish-black with white spot. Black central spot on forewing topside. Underside of hind wing white with irregular green markings, some yellowish. White sections sometimes nacreous (like mother-of-pearl). Front edge of hind wing set at obtuse angle by vein 8 (see no. 18a). Female similar to male, but bigger central spot on underside.

Distribution: Throughout southern Europe to 48°N, in lowlands and up to 1,500 m. Replaced at higher European altitudes by *ausonia ausonia*, with darker markings on forewings, and narrower central spot on topside of forewing merging with dark marking along wing edge. Also widespread in North Africa, through Asia to Amur region, and in North America.

Habitat: Grassy slopes and dry fields in lowland and lower mountains.

Life History: Two generations, on wing March–April and May–June. First generation sometimes very sparse in certain areas. Larva feeds on crucifers.

19 *Euchloe belemia*
Green-striped White

Characteristics: Male: Wing length 19–22 mm. Markings on topside very similar to *ausonia* (no. 18), but forewing more pointed, and

corner of hind wing at acute angle. Totally different underside of hind wing with clear transverse markings on green ground. Summer generation has lighter green ground colour than the spring. Female similar to male, but less pointed wings.

Distribution: Southern parts of Iberian Peninsula, especially Andalusia and south Portugal.

Habitat and Life History: Uncultivated land with wild herb vegetation from lowlands to 1,300 m. First generation on wing from late February to mid-April, second generation from late April to mid-June. Larva feeds on crucifers.

20 *Anthocharis belia euphenoides*
Morocco Orange Tip

Characteristics: Male: Wing length 18–20 mm. Topside yellow, broad orange band on forewing, lined with dark stripe through central spot; dark wing tip. Yellow underside, with extended grey markings on hind wings, especially in subbasal and discal sections; white post-discal spots in cells 2–7. Topside of female forewing whitish with wing tip spot of grey lines along veins interspersed with orange. Topside of hind wing more yellow. Underside similar to male.

Distribution: Most of Portugal and Spain. Also southernmost France, especially Provence, and locally in Switzerland and Italy (Mari-

time Alps, southern Alps and Apennines). The subspecies, *belia belia*, found in North Africa.
Habitat and Life History: Mainly mountainous areas, in Spain and Portugal to about 2,000 m. On wing from early March to mid-July. Visits flowers of various buckles mustard (*Biscutella*) species, which are also food plants of the larva.

21 *Anthocharis cardamines*
Orange Tip
Characteristics: Male: Wing length 19–24 mm. White topside, broad orange band with small black spot on forewing. Wing tip and border have narrow grey-brown marking. Underside of hind wing mottled white with irregular, merging yellowish-green markings; similar marking on tip of forewing. The female (no. 21a) lacks orange band, has larger black spot, and hardly any markings on underside of forewing. Underside of hind wing similar to male.
Distribution: Europe, except southern Spain and Portugal, also northern Scotland, Scandinavia and Finland north of polar circle. Common in British Isles. Eastwards through temperate parts of Asia to China.
Habitat: Mainly damp areas alongside woods, light woods, and meadows rich in flowers. Up to 2,000 m in Alps.
Life History: On wing for couple of months between May and July,

depending on latitude. Eggs deposited on various crucifers. For larva: see no. 222.

22 *Zegris eupheme*
Sooty Orange Tip
Characteristics: Male: Wing length 23–25 mm. White ground on topside, curved dark central spot on forewing; dark grey wing tip section, flecked with white orange spot. Yellow underside of forewing tip. Underside of hind wing similar to Morocco Orange Tip (*Anthocharis belia euphenoides*) (no. 20). Female often bigger, with or without small orange spot on wing tip.
Distribution: Spain, south of Burgos and Zaragoza provinces. Also Morocco, Asia Minor, southern Soviet Union and Iran.
Habitat and Life History: On the wing in low-lying areas in southern Spain from April, further north and at higher altitudes on wing May–June. Found up to 1,500 m, on cultivated and uncultivated land. Has direct, fast flight. Larva lives on *Sinapis incana*.

23 *Colias phicomone*
Mountain Clouded Yellow
Characteristics: Male: Wing length 20–25 mm. Topside of forewing yellowish-green with strong, dark-grey dusting, especially at base of veins and along them. Forewing has broad, greyish-brown band with row of yellowish-green spots along border. Topside of hind

wing has similar markings, but even more greyish-green dust and yellow central spot. Underside of hind wing yellow with slight grey dust at basal and central sections, and clear yellow or red central spot. Female (no. 23a) has whiter-green topside, and fainter band along border of forewing. Considerable individual variation in colour of topside, extent of grey dust and rows of light spots.

Distribution: European mountain areas, in Alps as far east as Hohe Tauern, in north Carpathians, Pyrenees and Cantabrian mountains of northern Spain.

Habitat and Life History: Alps and north Carpathians between 900–2,500 m, in northern Spain above 2,000 m. Frequents sunny alpine meadows with rich herb vegetation. The single generation on wing June to August, depending on altitude. Rare second generations appear in September. Eggs deposited singly on topside of leaves of pea family, especially vetch (*Vicea*). Larva overwinters after casting its skin twice, fully grown following May or June. Butterfly appears after short pupal stage.

24 *Colias nastes werdandi*
Pale Arctic Clouded Yellow

Characteristics: Male: Wing length 22–24 mm. Whitish-yellow topside with greenish tint and less grey dust than no. 23. Row of light

spots along border of forewing less distinct towards inside. Topside of hind wing has small, yellow central spot. Female similar to male, but lighter ground, and more grey dust on topside of hind wing. Both sexes usually have rose pink collar.

Distribution: North Scandinavian mountains, approximately 66°–70°N. Also Novaya Zemlya and North America (Labrador and Rocky Mountains), as separate subspecies.

Habitat and Life History: Arctic mountain moors down to upper edge of birch wood zone. Single generation on wing June–July, with fast strong flight. Larva lives on mountain milk vetch (*Astragalus alpinus*) and overwinters fully-grown.

25 *Colias palaeno*
Moorland Clouded Yellow

Characteristics: Male: Wing length 25–27 mm. Pale brimstone yellow ground on topside. Broad band on forewing and narrower band on hind wing, dark along border, with red fringes. Small dark spot with light centre on forewing, and light central spot on hind wing. Pale yellow underside with grey-green dust and central spots similar to those on topside. The female (no. 25a) has whitish topside, and band along border less clear towards inside.

Distribution: From Scandinavia and central Europe through Soviet

Union to Japan. Not in British Isles, wide areas of western or southern Europe. Local and irregular in Denmark but widely distributed in Sweden, Norway and Finland.

Habitat: Prefers damp meadows, marshes, forest and moorland bogs. Subspecies *europome* found locally in raised bogs in central Europe.

Life History: Single generation on wing with its strong, steady flight, June-July, in hottest hours of day. Eggs deposited singly on bog whortleberry (*Vaccinium*). For larva: see no. 223.

26 *Colias crocea*
Clouded Yellow

Characteristics: Male: Wing length 23–27 mm. Orange topside of forewing with broad, black border band, crossed with yellow dust stripes along veins. Orange hind wing with pale yellowish-green inside edge; inside section of wing covered with greyish dust. Clear scent-scale spot near base of cell 9. Female (no. 26a) has yellow spots in cell 2 and near tip of black forewing band. Hind wing covered with yellowish-grey dust, big orange central spot and yellow spots in band along border. On both sexes orange underside of forewing with yellowish-green band along border; black spots in cells 1b, 2 and 3. Underside of hind wing yellowish-green with one large and one smaller white spot surrounded by red rings, also faint red post-discal spots. Whitish female variety, *helice*, also occurs.

Distribution and Habitat: Most parts of Europe, to approximately 60°N, but only as far north as Midlands in British Isles. Migration to southern and central Scandinavia and northern Germany in varying numbers. More regular in central and western Europe. Favours fields rich in flowers, and drier, open places. Total distribution stretches from Europe through western Asia to Iran.

Life History: This typical migrant normally only overwinters in Mediterranean countries, where several generations on wing April until late autumn. Immigration of spring generation into central Europe and on into northern Europe May–June, July–September for summer generation. 'Native' generation appears later in autumn in central and western Europe. Larva lives on lucerne (*Medicago*), vetch (*Vicea*) and other plants of pea family.

27 *Colias myrmidone*
Danube Clouded Yellow

Characteristics: Male: Wing length 22–25 mm. Very similar to no. 26, but slightly more reddish-orange ground on topside, smaller central spot on forewing, and infrequent clear dust stripes along veins 5–8 in dark band along border. Small black spots on underside of forewing in cells 1b, 2 and 3, if at all. Female (no. 27a) has prominent row of yellow spots on inside of band along hind wing border. Whitish females also found. Species shows considerable variation.

Distribution: East European steppe including south-east Germany as far as Munich environs; eastwards through Soviet Union to western Asia.

Habitat and Life History: Frequents heaths and other open, low-lying dry areas. Two generations: first on wing May–June, second July–September. Larva lives on broom (*Cytisus*).

28 *Colias hecla sulitelma*
Northern Clouded Yellow

Characteristics: Male: Wing length 20–23 mm. Orange topside of forewing, small central spot, fairly narrow dark border band striped with yellow. Central spot on hind wing is white with red ring. The female (no. 28a) has brimstone yellow spots in border band of forewing, and similar spots along inside edge of hind wing border. Extensive grey dust on hind wing.

Distribution and Habitat: Scandinavia and Finland, north of 68°N. Also Greenland, North America and arctic Asia. Frequents mountain heaths at lower altitudes in north than in south.

Life History: Single generation, on wing June–July, often abundant. Butterfly visits flowers of mountain milk vetch (*Astragalus alpinus*) among others, depositing eggs in small groups on leaves. Larva takes two years to develop.

29 *Colias hyale*
Pale Clouded Yellow

Characteristics: Male: Wing length 21–25 mm. Pale yellow topside, broad black border band broken by yellowish spots on forewing, narrow irregular border band near tip of hind wing. Both wings have red fringes. Only faint dusting near base of wing. Female (no. 29a) whiter with yellowish-green tinge; otherwise similar to male. Both sexes have faint orange central spot on hind wing. Difficult to distinguish from *Colias australis*, brighter yellow, with less distinct dark border markings, and less shading at base of forewing.

Distribution: Western and central Europe and through southern Soviet Union to Altai mountains. southern British Isles. Sometimes great numbers of migrants on German and Dutch North Sea coast, in Denmark, southern and central Sweden and Finland (see below). Probably replaced in Italy and Iberian Peninsula by *australis*.

Habitat: Flowering lucerne and clover fields, also gravel pits, railway embankments, and road sides with wild flowers.

Life History: Two to three merging generations in central Europe on wing May until late autumn. Larva lives on plants of pea family, such as clover (*Trifolium*), lucerne (*Medicago*), milk vetch (*Vicea*) and *Coronilla*. Larva green with yellow or reddish side stripes. Larva of last generation overwinters. Green pupa is fixed to plant stem.

30 *Gonepteryx rhamni*
Brimstone
Characteristics: Male: Wing length 26–30 mm. Yellow ground both sides; small, orange central spots. Border of forewing concave near front; hind wing has obtuse angle at rib 3. Topside of female (no. 30a) white with faint yellow-green tinge; underside of hind wing and front part of forewing yellower. Hibernating individuals often have brown spots along edge of wing.
Distribution: Most of Europe. Northern limit in Norway, approximately 61°N, in Sweden and Finland 64°N–65°N. Through Soviet Union and Asia Minor to Siberia, also North Africa.
Habitat: Common in southern British Isles in woods, gardens, on roadsides with flowers. Elsewhere to 2,000 m.
Life History: Butterfly very long-lived, hatching from pupa in June-July; after 8–10 days begins summer hibernation, interrupted by short autumn flying period in August–September, before true hibernation. Overwinters in ever-green bushes or on ground in woods among leaves and grass. On wing again in early spring; after mating, female deposits eggs

April–May on underside of leaves of alder buckthorn or common buckthorn (*Rhamnus frangula* and *Rhamnus carthartica*). For larva: see no. 224.

31 *Gonepteryx cleopatra*
Cleopatra
Characteristics: Male: Wing length 25–30 mm. Similar to no. 30, except for large orange section on topside of forewing. Underside pale greenish-yellow. Female similar to no. 30a, but with orange line on underside of fore-wing.
Distribution: Spain, Portugal, southern France and Italy, as far north as southern alpine valleys. Also North Africa, Greece and parts of Near East.
Habitat and Life History: Mainly mountain slopes with open wood and scrub. Single generation on wing from June. Hibernates like previous species. Larva lives on *Rhamnus* species.

32 *Leptidea sinapis*
Wood White
Characteristics: Male: Wing length 19–24 mm. Chalk-white ground on topside, with grey or black spot on tip, darkest on second generation. Underside yellowish-white or yellowish-green with varying amount of greyish dusting, less on second generation. Females (no. 32a) of first generation have grey stripes along veins at wing tip, while second generation females

have very faint wing tip spot, or none at all.

Distribution: Most of Europe, except Dutch–German North Sea coast, western Denmark, southern British Isles (but not common), and north-western Scandinavia and Finland. Also Soviet Russia to Caucasus. Not North Africa.

Habitat: Mainly forest clearings and edge of forests.

Life History: Usually on the wing in May–June and July–August respectively. Flight low and irregular. Eggs deposited on underside of leaves of everlasting pea (*Lathyrus*), milk vetch (*Vicea*), birdsfoot-trefoil (*Lotus*) and other plants of pea family. Slim larva measures 20 mm long, pale green with yellow side stripes. Eats leaves of host plant for about one month before pupation and overwintering.

LIBYTHEIDAE

This small family consists of about ten similar widespread species characterised by their long labial palps and deeply serrated wing border. Males have reduced forelegs like Nymphalidae species. Many species are migrants.

33 *Libythea celtis*
Nettle-tree Butterfly

Characteristics: Male: Wing length 17–22 mm. Easily distinguished from other European butterflies by prominent point on border of forewing. Topside dark brown with orange markings, with whitish double spot near edge of forewing. Underside of forewing similar to topside. Underside of hind wing brownish and greyish, with occasional white line. Female similar.

Distribution: Iberian Peninsula through southern France and Italy (as far north as southern alpine valleys), through southern valleys of Austria and Balkans to Asia Minor, Siberia and Japan. Also North Africa.

Habitat and Life History: Up to about 500 m where host plant, nettle tree (*Celtis australis*), grows. Newly-hatched butterflies on wing June to September. Overwinter until March–April following year, when they mate and deposit eggs.

NYMPHALIDAE (BROWNS)

By far the largest butterfly family, comprising many thousand species distributed worldwide. In its broader definition includes the sub-families Nymphalinae, also Satyridae and Charaxinae.

Mostly medium-sized or big butterflies, with reduced forelegs, at least in the male. Nymphalidae larvae vary considerably. Pupae are normally suspended by hooks (cremasters), on the hind end.

34 *Apatura iris*
Purple Emperor
Characteristics: Male: Wing length 31–37 mm. Ground of topside is brownish-black, reflecting purple over most of surface with its white bands and spots. Forewing has faint black spot in cell 2. Underside has very clear reddish-brown, greyish-brown and white markings. Black ocellus (eye spot) with blue centre on orange ground in cell 2 on forewing. White band with straight inside edge on underside of hind wing. Female (no. 34a) larger, with no purple reflections on topside.
Distribution: Western Europe (including southern British Isles) through central and eastern Europe to temperate areas of Asia. Northern limit in Denmark and Baltic States about 60°N. Also northern Portugal and certain mountain areas in northern Spain. Not Scandinavia, but occasional immigrants in Finland.
Habitat: Old mixed hardwood forests up to 1,000 m.

Life History: Flight easy and elegant, among topmost branches of trees, where male guards territory. Comes down to drink, especially in morning. Single generation on wing July–August. Eggs deposited singly on topside of leaves of willow (*Salix*), especially goat willow (*Salix caprea*). Overwinters completely exposed, on twigs of foodplant. For larva: see no. 225.

35 *Apatura ilia*
Small Purple Emperor
Characteristics: Male: Wing length 32–35 mm. Similar to no. 34, with purple reflection on topside. Orange ring encircles black spot in cell 2 of forewing. Underside markings less clear, especially on hind wing, with its blurred white band and wavy inside edge. Female is bigger with no purple reflection. Both sexes may have yellowish-brown topside.
Distribution: France, Belgium through central, eastern and southern Europe, and eastwards

through temperate zone of Asia to Japan. Sporadic in northern Spain and Portugal. Unique occurrence in Finland.
Habitat and Life History: Like Purple Emperor (no. 34), frequents hardwood forests. Two generations in south, on wing May–June and August–September. Further north single generation, on wing July. Otherwise very similar to Purple Emperor. Larva lives on poplar (*Populus*) and willow (*Salix*) species.

36 *Neptis rivularis*
Hungarian Glider
Characteristics: Male and female: Wing length 25–27 mm. Topside brownish-black with extensive white markings, forming single diagonal discal band, crossed by black veins on hind wing. Underside predominantly cinnamon-brown with markings similar to topside.
Distribution: Southern alpine valleys in Switzerland and South Tyrol; from eastern Alps and Austria to Hungary and Czechoslovakia, and eastwards through southern Soviet Union to central Asia. Not British Isles.
Habitat and Life History: Isolated colonies in forest clearings up to 1,000 m. Single generation on wing with slow, hovering flight in June and July. Larva lives on *Spiraea* species. Overwinters and fully grown by May.

37 *Charaxes jasius*
Two-tailed Pasha
Characteristics: Male: Wing length 38–41 mm. Topside dark brown; broad, yellowish-brown marginal band on forewing with yellowish-brown post-discal spots becoming less clear towards back. Yellowish-brown marginal band continues on hind wing, edged with black and blue spots in cells 1–4. Two short tails on hind wing. Underside (no. 37a) has complex pattern of white transverse band outside irregular reddish-brown spots edged with white and set on brown ground. Female larger, but otherwise similar.
Distribution: Along Mediterranean coast from Portugal and Spain through southern France and Italian west coast to Balkans; also many Mediterranean islands and Africa.
Habitat and Life History: Mainly near coasts, but also up to 800 m. Local and rare in most places. Two generations, the first on wing May–June, second more abundant, on wing August–September. Males particularly mobile with very rapid flight. Larva lives on strawberry tree (*Arbutus unedo*).

38 *Limenitis populi*
Poplar Admiral
Characteristics: Male: Wing length 35–40 mm. Topside dark brown with greyish tint. White spots, sometimes faint, in central cell and post-discal sections. Orange

and black sub-marginal spots more or less intense. Underside (no. 38a) basically orange, with white or bluish-grey markings and rows of dark spots. Female larger with whiter topside.

Distribution: From France through central and eastern Europe to Japan. South-east Norway, up to 64°N in Sweden and about 65°N in Finland. Very rare in western France, Holland, north-west Germany and Denmark.

Habitat: Open, damp forest clearings.

Life History: Single generation on wing in July. Favours carrion, horse manure and other pungent matter. Easiest to find early in the day before it flies to tree tops. Eggs deposited on topside of lower leaves of aspen (*Populus tremula*) and other poplar species. Young larva overwinters on twig. In spring feeds on fresh leaves; fully-grown by May–June, about 50 mm long, and green with dark spots. Two rows of spines on back and luminescent spots on sides of segments 5 and 7. Brownish-yellow with peculiar hump, pupa is attached to leaf. After 14 days butterfly emerges from pupal stage.

39 *Limenitis camilla*
White Admiral
Characteristics: Male: Wing length 26–30 mm. Topside brownish-black with white markings, very faint spot in central cell of fore-

wing, if present at all (cf. no. 40). Underside (no. 39a) basically brown and yellowish-brown, with white markings similar to those on topside, and bluish-grey near base and inner edge of hind wing, with its two rows of small, black spots. Female similar.

Distribution: Southern British Isles and France, through central and eastern Europe and eastwards through Soviet Union and central Asia to China and Japan. Northern limit through north-west Germany, Denmark and southern Sweden. Not in Norway or Finland. One of few species re-establishing in southern British Isles, notably Forest of Dean.

Habitat: Damp hardwood forests.

Life History: Single generation, on wing with its fairly low, slow flight from late June to late July. Butterfly prefers semi-shade under trees and frequents flowers, especially of blackberry. Larva (no. 226) lives on honeysuckle (*Lonicera*) species.

40 *Limenitis reducta*
Southern White Admiral
Characteristics: Male: Wing length 23–27 mm. Similar to no. 39, apart from bluish-black tint in ground on topside, especially along border. Clear, white spot in central cell, black spots with blue edges near border on fore- and hind wings, and single row of small, black spots on underside of hind wing also distinguish this

species from White Admiral. Female similar.

Distribution: Further south than White Admiral: in central Europe to about 50°N; rare in western and northern France, unknown in British Isles and northern Europe. In southern Europe, through Balkans and southern Soviet Union to Caucasus and Iran.

Habitat and Life History: Like two previous *Limenitis* species, *reducta* frequents damp forest areas. In southern Europe one or two generations, on wing May–June and July–September. North of Alps single generation on wing mid-June to mid-July. Larva lives on honeysuckle (*Lonicera*), overwintering in small web in angle between two branches.

41 *Nymphalis antiopa*
Camberwell Beauty
Characteristics: Male: Wing length 30–34 mm. Very dark topside with purple tinge. Both wings have broad, yellowish border bands, almost white during hibernation. Row of blue spots inside border band. Female similar.

Distribution: Most of Europe, except southern Spain and Mediterranean islands. In British Isles rare immigrant on coast. Throughout Scandinavia and Finland, to North Cape, also North America and temperate areas of Asia. Population fluctuates, especially in northern and western distribution areas.

Habitat: Forest clearings and open woods. Species migrates over long distances so presence does not necessarily indicate local breeding.

Life History: Single generation annually, on wing from June–July till late autumn, and again in spring after hibernation, visiting trees. Flight is elegant and strong. Feeds on sap and fermenting fruit. Female deposits 200–250 eggs April–May in sleeve round thin branches, notably of birch (*Betula*) and willow (*Salix*). For larva: see no. 227.

42 *Nymphalis polychloros*
Large Tortoiseshell
Characteristics: Male: Wing length 25–32 mm. Orange-brown topside with dark markings. Black border on forewing with light crescent-shaped spots; hind wing band has blue crescent-shaped spots. Narrow, distinct black rim inside blue spots. Underside light brown to brownish black, lightest in post-discal sections. Distinguished from no. 43 by very dark hair on palps and legs.

Distribution: North Africa, southern and central Europe, including south-east British Isles, through central and southern Soviet Union to Himalayas. Northern limit south-east Norway through central Sweden to south-west Finland. European population declining; very sporadic in North Europe.

Habitat: Open, slightly damp, sunny places in forests, parks or gardens with elm and willow.

Life History: On wing June–July till late summer and April–May after hibernation. Eggs deposited in groups on outermost branches of fruit trees (apple, pear, cherry), elm (*Ulmus*), willow (*Salix*) and poplar (*Populus*). Larvae live socially in loose web surrounding top branches. Fully grown within a month, 40 mm long, black with bluish or brownish velvety hair, and about 70 yellow, pointed spines and many small, white warts. Larvae fall to ground singly and pupate on vertical objects at fairly low height. Butterfly emerges after two weeks.

43 *Nymphalis xanthomelas*
Yellow-legged Tortoiseshell
Characteristics: Male and female: Wing length 30–32 mm. Very similar to previous species, but border of forewing more prominently pointed, black rim inside blue crescent-shaped spots on hind wing broader and less clearly defined towards inside. Legs and palps covered with yellowish hair.
Distribution and Habitat: Southeast Europe and locally but rare in central Europe. Occasionally Denmark, southern Sweden and southern Finland on late summer migration.
Life History: See no. 42. Usual host trees are willow species (*Salix*), where larvae spin large, characteristic nests.

44 *Inachis io*
Peacock
Characteristics: Male: Wing length 27–29 mm. Big ocelli on topsides of forewing and hind wing. Underside very dark. Female slightly larger.
Distribution: Throughout Europe; north to about 61°N in Scandinavia, southern Finland, and temperate zone of Asia to Japan. Particularly common in southern British Isles.
Habitat: Open, sunny places with flowers, gardens, roadsides, forest clearings, up to 2,500 m.
Life History: Newly-hatched individuals on wing from late July to late autumn. Overwinter in lofts, sheds and hollow trees; on wing again in spring. Eggs deposited in terminal shoots of nettles (*Urtica dioica*), often in batches of several hundred. For larva: see no. 228.

45 *Polygonia c-album*
Comma
Characteristics: Male and female: Wing length 22–24 mm. Sharply serrated wing border. Topside orange-brown with dark brown markings. Underside (no. 45a) mottled light and dark brown. C-shaped marking on hind wing. In south-east France and Italy species *Polygonia egea* found with Y-shaped spot on underside of hind wing and lighter topside.
Distribution: Southern and central Sweden along east coast to Finnish

border, southern Norway, and western and southern Finland. Increasing in southern British Isles; fairly sporadic in north-west Europe, including Denmark. Found through Asia to China and Japan.
Habitat: Forest clearings and woodland meadows.
Life History: The two generations on wing June–July and July–September. Overwintered individuals of second generation also seen in spring. The butterfly is a good flier. Eggs deposited singly on nettle (*Urtica*), elm (*Ulmus*), willow (*Salix*), hop (*Humulus*) and others. Larva lives singly in light web on back of leaves. Pupates on host plant. Pupal stage lasts 2–3 weeks.

46 *Vanessa atalanta*
Red Admiral
Characteristics: Male and female: Wing length 28–31 mm. Topside brownish-black, red band across central cell to bottom corner of forewing and white spots on tip. Red border band in cells 2–5 on hind wing. Underside of forewing similar to topside. Underside of hind wing mottled dark and light brown.
Distribution and Habitat: Throughout Europe up to 62°N, on annual migration from south, reaching British Isles in July. Migrants deposit eggs, and native generation on wing in August; quite mobile and widespread.

Frequents flowers in gardens and edge of woods.
Life History: Native generation on wing in British Isles till late October. Summer generation overwinters in southern Europe and does not survive in British Isles. Red Admirals migrate singly, so difficult to observe. Eggs deposited singly in July on nettle (*Urtica*). For larva: see no. 229.

47 *Vanessa cardui*
Painted Lady
Characteristics: Male and female: Wing length 27–29 mm. Yellowish-brown topside with brownish-black markings and white spots on tip of forewing. Five small ocelli on underside of hind wing (no. 47a).
Distribution and Habitat: Throughout Europe with spring migration in varying numbers from North Africa where it is on wing all year. Migrants produce native generations in summer, but hibernation not normal north of Alps. Range includes northernmost Scandinavia, but breeding not normal in north. Frequents open land, preferably dry places with flowers.
Life History: Single native generation in British Isles, two in central Europe, three further south. Native generation on wing till September together with second generation migrants from south. Solitary larva lives on various thistle species, feeding under a web, low down. Similar to Red Admiral.

48 *Aglais urticae*
Small Tortoiseshell
Characteristics: Male: Wing length 22–25 mm. Yellowish-orange topside with broad dark basal section on hind wing; black and yellow spots on forewing. Border band on hind wing with small, blue spots. Underside of hind wing brownish-black at base, with lighter brown post-discal section and dark brown border band. Female similar, but slightly larger.
Distribution: Throughout Europe, Soviet Union and Asia. Not North Africa.
Habitat: Open places with flower vegetation up to 3,000 m.
Life History: In northern Europe single generation on wing late June till October; two generations in British Isles. Overwinters in sheds and lofts, on wing again in early spring, when mating takes place. Eggs deposited in clumps on terminal shoots of nettle (*Urtica dioica*). For larva: see no. 230.

49 *Argynnis paphia*
Silver-washed Fritillary
Characteristics: Male: Wing length 27–35 mm. Topside yellowish-brown with black stripes and spots, distinct scent-scale stripes on veins 1–4. Underside of forewing (no. 49a) paler yellowish-brown with some green at tips. Underside of hind wing greenish with silvery transverse bands and border band; violet tint in post-discal section. Two different colour forms of

female, one similar to male, but without scent-scale stripes and with larger dark spots; other form has olive-coloured topside.
Distribution: Most of Europe except southern Spain and Portugal, in Scandinavia as far north as 63°N, and south-west British Isles. Also temperate areas of Asia as far east as Japan.
Habitat: Forest areas.
Life History: On wing mid-July to August. Female deposits eggs in cracks in bark of oak and fir trees. On hatching, larva crawls down to feed on violets. See also: no. 232.

50 *Pandoriana pandora*
Cardinal
Characteristics: Male: Wing length 32–40 mm. Topside yellowish-brown with varying amount of greenish tint. Distinct scent-scale stripes along veins 2 and 3. Underside of forewing (no. 50a) rose-pink near base, greenish near tip. Underside of hind wing greenish with silvery stripes and small, white post-discal spots. Female (no. 50) bigger, with clear greyish-green tint.
Distribution and Habitat: Portugal and Spain through southern France and Italy to Balkans, as far north as southern alpine valleys, lower Austria and Moravia. Also North Africa. Frequents meadows with flowers.
Life History: In Europe on wing June–July. Like larva of Silver-

washed Fritillary (no. 49), Cardinal larva lives on violet species.

51 *Araschnia levana*
Map Butterfly
Characteristics: Male and female: Wing length 16–19 mm. Two widely different forms. Spring generation (*levana*, no. 51) yellowish-brown with dark markings and small, white post-discal spots. Underside reddish-brown with intricate light stripes and spots. Summer generation (*prorsa*, no. 51a) brownish-black with light post-discal bands. Underside similar to *levana*.
Distribution: France through central and eastern Europe, as far north as Baltic countries. Also Denmark, eastern Finland, parts of southern Europe and through Soviet Union and Asia to Japan.
Habitat: Open forest areas.
Life History: Spring generation on wing June–July, summer generation July–August. Eggs suspended like small rows of pearls on underside of nettle (*Urtica*) leaves, 7–8 eggs in each row, with only first egg fixed to leaf. For larva: see no. 231.

52 *Mesoacidalia aglaja*
Dark Green Fritillary
Characteristics: Male: Wing length 24–29 mm. Small post-discal spot in cell 4 on hind wing. Silvery basal, discal, and marginal spots on underside of hind wing (no. 52a), but no post-discal spots

(cf. no. 53a). Underside otherwise light yellowish-brown with green sections on hind wing. Female slightly paler on topside.
Distribution: Throughout Europe and Asia to Japan. Locally common in southern British Isles.
Habitat: Mainly woodland meadows up to timber line.
Life History: Single generation on wing June–July. Eggs deposited 2 or 3 together on violet species. For larva: see no. 233.

53 *Fabriciana adippe*
High Brown Fritillary
Characteristics: Male: Wing length 25–31 mm. This species and no. 54 distinguished from no. 52 by small reddish silver-centred post-discal spots on underside of hind wing (see 53a and 54a). *Adippe* usually lacks this spot in cell 4 and dark spot in cell 4 on topside. Male has distinct scent-scale stripes along veins 2 and 3 on forewing, unlike female.
Distribution: Most of Europe, (except northern British Isles); in Scandinavia and Finland as far as 62°–63°N. Subspecies, *chlorodippe*, found in Spain. Also found through Asia to Japan.
Habitat and Life History: Frequents woodland meadows up to timber line. On wing June–July. Larva lives on sweet violet (*Viola odorata*) and other violet species. Overwinters and reaches maturity in two spring months.

54 *Fabriciana niobe*
Niobe Fritillary
Characteristics: Male: Wing length
23–30 mm. Very narrow scent-
scale stripes along veins 2 and 3,
small, but distinct post-discal spot
in cell 4 of hind wing. Underside
of hind wing (no. 54a) greenish
near base, small post-discal spot
in cell 4, normally clear, often
without centre. Veins pronounced.
Female has paler ground with
stronger markings.
Distribution: Almost same areas as
no. 53, but absent from British
Isles and certain Mediterranean
islands. Occurs through Soviet
Union and Asia Minor to Iran.
Habitat and Life History: Niobe
found on poorer soil than *adippe*.
The single annual generation on
wing June–August. For larva: see
no. 234.

55 *Issoria lathonia*
**Queen of Spain
Fritillary**
Characteristics: Male and female:
Wing length 19–23 mm. Relatively
shorter and more pointed wings
than three previous species, with
more prominent corner of forewing. Enormous silvery spots on
underside of hind wing (no. 55a).
Distribution: Most of Europe, but
rare visitors to British Isles. In
Scandinavia to 62°–64°N, but
only migrants in northern areas.
Central Asia to western China.
Habitat and Life History: Dry
places with little or no vegetation;

enjoys sunshine. Visits flowers,
especially daisy (*Compositae*)
species. First summer generation
on wing May–June, second
August–September, sometimes
swelled in number by migrants.
Single generation in north, three
in south. Larvae of summer
generation overwinter. Live on
violet and pansy species.

56 *Brenthis hecate*
Twin-spot Fritillary
Characteristics: Male and female:
Wing length 18–22 mm. Two
complete, uniform rows of dark
post-discal and sub-marginal spots
on topside. Underside of hind wing
(no. 56a) has yellow and brown
pattern, sections edged with dark;
two prominent rows of dark spots.
Female has darker base.
Distribution: Mountain areas in
southern and central Spain, southern France, and Po valley in
Italy; through Balkans to Asia
Minor and central Asia.
Habitat and Life History: Uncultivated slopes and woodland
meadows. On wing June–July.
Larva's host plant unknown, and
various development stages un-
documented.

57 *Brenthis daphne*
Marbled Fritillary
Characteristics: Male and female:
Wing length 21–26 mm. Similar
to no. 56, but post-discal spots
on forewing not uniform. Underside of hind wing (57a) less clearly

marked, broad post-discal section marbled brown and violet, without distinct spots.

Distribution: Southern Europe from north-east Spain and southern and eastern France through southern alpine valleys and Italy to Balkans (as far north as Austria, Czechoslovakia and Hungary). Through Soviet Union and central Asia to Japan.

Habitat and Life History: Local and fairly rare in western part of range. Prefers warm valleys on wing June till late August. Larva lives on bramble (*Rubus*) species and violets. Overwinters August to May.

58 *Brenthis ino*
Lesser Marbled Fritillary

Characteristics: Male: Wing length 17–20 mm. Noticeably smaller than no. 57. Post-discal spots on topside vary in size. Marginal band, more complete, especially on hind wing. Underside of hind wing (58a) has more or less distinct violet band, irregular post-discal spots and ocelli. Female slightly bigger, topside often covered with darker dust, but lighter ground.

Distribution: Northern Spain and France through central and northern Europe, eastwards through temperate areas of Asia to Japan. Not northern France, British Isles, western and northern Scandinavia, or most of southern Europe.

Habitat and Life History: Exclusively in damp places rich in vegetation, boggy meadows, along streams and in damp, open woodland. Often very limited. Numbers fluctuate considerably. Single generation on wing June–August. Eggs deposited on underside of the leaves of spiraea (*Filipendula*) and raspberry among other *Rubus* species. For larva: see no. 235.

59 *Boloria napaea*
Mountain Fritillary

Characteristics: Male and female: Wing length 17–23 mm. Delicate striped dark spot on topside. Extensive dark marking on basal section of hind wing. Underside of forewing (no. 59a) very blurred. Underside of hind wing subtle mixture of yellowish-green and reddish-grey.

Distribution: Scandinavian mountains from 60°N to North Cape, Alps and eastern Pyrenees. Unknown in British Isles.

Habitat and Life History: Damp grassland at or above timber line, in Alps from 1,500 to 3,000 m. Single generation on wing July–August. Host plants of larva mainly violet species. Larva overwinters twice, second time in light web.

60 *Boloria aquilonaris*
Cranberry Fritillary

Characteristics: Male and female: Wing length 16–17 mm. Well-developed spots on underside of forewing (no. 60a). Reddish-grey, reddish-brown and yellow markings on underside of hind wing. Indistinct reddish-brown post-discal band cuts between yellow spot in cell 3 and margin. Six silvery marginal spots, and other silvery spots in outer part of central cell, in cell 7, and cell 1c near back corner. Female often covered with dark dust.

Distribution: Mainly Scandinavia and Finland. Also parts of central Europe (Poland, Czechoslovakia, Austria and Germany). Isolated populations in Belgium and central France. Not British Isles.

Habitat: Quagmires with sphagnum moss, rather scattered and restricted.

Life History: Single generation on wing June–July. Larva lives on cranberry (*Oxycoccus palustris*) April–May, having overwintered in sphagnum. Eats only on warm days. Pupa suspended in sphagnum.

61 *Proclossiana eunomia*
Bog Fritillary

Characteristics: Male and female: Wing length 20–23 mm. No sharp colour contrasts on underside of hind wing (no. 61a), but sections clearly marked with dark lines. Narrow, blurred post-discal band has six black rings filled with white. Female often has brown dust on topside.

Distribution and Habitat: Scattered localities in western and central Europe, in bogs and damp meadows from lowlands to 1,700 m. Not Denmark, north-west Germany, Holland or British Isles. In Scandinavia and Finland several subspecies found locally in bogs, mainly in lowlands. Scandinavian specimens usually darker with silvery marginal spots. *Life History:* On wing June–August, with rapid and unsteady flight. Larva lives on bog whortle-berry and other *Vaccinium* species, also snakeweed (*Polygonum bistorta*). Takes two years to develop.

62 *Clossiana selene*
Small Pearl-bordered Fritillary

Characteristics: Male and female: Wing length 18–21 mm. Topside orange-brown with extensive black markings on Scandinavian species (no. 62), while central European species less distinctly marked. Underside (no. 62a) dark reddish-brown, with interrupted post-discal band on hind wing, and marginal spots on hind wing clearly defined towards inside by acute, black angles.

Distribution: Widespread in western, central and northern Europe. Not Spain, except north-west, nor Italy or southern Balkans. Northern and central Asia, also North America.

Habitat and Life History: Woodland meadows and damp grassland with many flowers. Two generations in southern British Isles, on wing June–July and August respectively. Second generation smaller. In mountain areas, northern Scandinavia and northern England. Single generation on wing June–July. Thimble-shaped eggs deposited singly on flowers or leaves of violet species; larvae appear late June. Overwinter in dead leaves, then eat and reach maturity following spring.

63 *Clossiana euphrosyne*
Pearl-bordered Fritillary

Characteristics: Male and female: Wing length 19–23 mm. Topside similar to previous species. Underside of hind wing (no. 64a) has lighter reddish-brown post-discal band, and less clearly defined marginal spots towards the inside than no. 62.

Distribution: Most of Europe; north west Iberian Peninsula, southern British Isles and throughout northern Asia to Pacific.

Habitat: Woodland and meadows, dry fields, heaths, up to about 2,000 m.

Life History: Two generations on wing April–May and July–August in southern areas. Single generation on wing May–June in north. Eggs deposited on leaves of violet species, especially sweet violet. After third change of skin larva hibernates on underside of dead leaf. Larval stage lasts about 10 months, pupal stage only couple of weeks.

64 *Clossiana titania cypris*
Titania's Fritillary

Characteristics: Male and female: Wing length 21–24 mm. Underside of hind wing (no. 64a) dark, with reddish-violet, brown and yellow markings. Black post-discal spots very close to black angular spots inside margin. Topside of female lighter than male.

Distribution: Southern and central Alps north to Bavaria, east to Austria, southern Finland and east Baltic countries. Also Siberia and North America. Unknown in British Isles.

Habitat and Life History: Like no. 63, prefers open woodland, up to 1,200–1,700 m in Alps. Frequents northern European lowlands. On wing June–July. Larva overwinters on violets (*Viola*) and knotgrass (*Polygonum*).

65 *Clossiana freija*
Frejya's Fritillary

Characteristics: Male and female: Wing length 18–22 mm. Extensive dark dust on wing base of topside. Underside of hind wing (no. 65a) characteristic black zigzag at back of discal section; hind wing marbled in light and dark brown with white markings and large marginal spots.

Distribution: In Europe only in Norway and Sweden north of 60°N. Northern Siberia to Japan and North America.

Habitat and Life History: On wing briefly in June and early July in areas of bogs and mountains. Flight low, not particularly rapid. Larva lives on cloudberry (*Rubus chamaemorus*) and bog whortleberry (*Vaccinium uliginosum*). Not well documented.

66 *Clossiana chariclea*
Arctic Fritillary
Characteristics: Male and female: Wing length 16–18 mm. Topside very similar to *freija* (no. 65). Underside of hind wing has prominent whitish discal band with silvery spots. Underside reddish-brown to light brownish-yellow in post-discal section. Marginal spots often silvery.
Distribution and Habitat: Arctic and subarctic Scandinavia and Finland, in dry tundra fields and boggy areas. Also Greenland and North America.
Life History: On wing July–August, in warmest hours of day. Often rests on stones warming itself in the sun. Larva unknown.

67 *Clossiana improba*
Dusky-winged Fritillary
Characteristics: Male and female: Wing length 15–17 mm. Easily recognised by dark topside with no distinct markings. Underside of hind wing brownish with light discal band and clear white spots in cells 4 and 7. Small, white rim along front edge.
Distribution: Like *improba* (no. 66), only Norway, Sweden and Finland, in mountains at about

68°–69°N. Also North America and Novaya Zemlya.
Habitat and Life History: Mountain areas; dry places with scattered grasses, lichen and other vegetation. On wing in July; more males than females in evidence. Larva apparently lives on dwarf willow (*Salix herbacea*).

68 *Clossiana dia*
Violet Fritillary
Characteristics: Male and female: Wing length 16–17 mm. Distinguishable from other European *Clossiana* species by acute angle between margin and front edge on hind wing. Underside of hind wing (no. 68a) mainly violet-brown with silvery discal spots in cells 1c, 4 and 7, also small, silvery marginal spots. Distinct dark spots in post-discal section.
Distribution: From France through central and eastern Europe and central Asia to China.
Habitat and Life History: Light, open woods, meadows and heaths. Up to about 1,200 m in Alps. Two or three generations on wing late April to late October. Larva lives on violet species, *Rubus* species (such as blackberry and raspberry) and other plants. Half-grown larva overwinters. Larvae of first and second generations sometimes overwinter together.

69 *Clossiana thore*
Thor's Fritillary
Characteristics: Male: Wing length

20–23 mm. Rather blurred dark markings on topside. Characteristic, brimstone-yellow discal band on underside of hind wing (no. 69a). Female larger with lighter topside.

Distribution: Alps of Switzerland, Germany, Austria and Italy at heights of 700–2,000 m, also Scandinavian and Finnish mountains above 62°N. Also through Soviet Union and Asia to Japan.

Habitat and Life History: Mountain valleys and grassland in birch zone. Single generation on wing late June and July. Butterfly visits flowers and suns itself on leaves. In Alps larva lives on violet species, but host plants for larva of Scandinavian populations unknown. Larva believed to hibernate through two winters.

70 *Clossiana frigga*
Frigg's Fritillary

Characteristics: Male and female: Wing length 20–25 mm. Topside has heavy, dark marking on basal and discal sections, especially on hind wing. Underside of hind wing (no. 70a) reddish-brown near base with lighter discal band with whitish spots in cells 4 and 7.

Distribution: Scandinavia and Finland especially north of about 60°N; not western Norway or British Isles. Through northern Asia to North America.

Habitat and Life History: Bogs and damp meadows. On wing June–July. Larva apparently lives on willow (*Salix*) and overwinters.

71 *Melitaea cinxia*
Glanville Fritillary

Characteristics: Male: Wing length 14–20 mm. Characteristic small, black spots on hind wing within row of yellow-brown spots in submarginal section. Yellow-brown submarginal band on underside of hind wing (no. 71a) defined towards inside by black inward concave arches. Marginal spots small, black and distinct. Female bigger and darker.

Distribution: Most of Europe, not southern Spain nor British Isles, except colony on Isle of Wight. Northern limit Scandinavia and Finland around 60°N. Eastwards to northern Asia.

Habitat and Life History: Open places rich in flowers, often near woods, also meadows and roadsides. Single generation on wing in June; two generations in southern Europe. Eggs deposited in clumps on underside of leaves of plantain species (*Plantago*), more rarely hawkweed (*Hieracium*) and other plants. Larvae live socially in web where they hibernate. In spring live singly. Pupae sit on stones and stems. Butterfly emerges after 3 weeks.

72 *Melitaea phoebe phoebe*
Knapweed Fritillary

Characteristics: Male and female: Wing length 18–25 mm. Topside of hind wing has orange-brown submarginal spots, normally without black centres. Submarginal band of hind wing yellow on underside (no. 72a) edged with black crescent-shaped lines; orange spot in each cell. Considerable variation.

Distribution: Southern and central Europe to about 50°N (central Germany). Subspecies *occitanica* found in Spain and Portugal. Topside of *occitanica*'s wing has submarginal band with brighter contrasts of colour. Also central Asia to northern China.

Habitat and Life History: From lowlands to more than 2,000 m in Alps. Prefers meadows and slopes with rich flower vegetation. North of Alps single generation on wing May–July. In southern Europe 2 or 3 generations. Larva overwinters on knapweed (*Centaurea*) species.

73 *Melitaea didyma meridionalis*
Spotted Fritillary
Characteristics: Male and female: Wing length 18–23 mm. Most variable European butterfly. Illustrations here show males of most common southern European subspecies, *meridionalis*, with dark orange-brown topside, and black post-discal spots rather blurred towards front. Underside of hind wing (no. 73a) has orange bands near base and in submarginal section. Topside of females usually dusted heavy dark grey.

Distribution: Southern and central Europe through Soviet Union to central Asia. The northern Europ-

ean limit from north-west France and Belgium through central Germany to north-east Poland. Not British Isles, Denmark, northern Germany or Holland.

Habitat and Life History: Like no. 72, found in open, sunny places with flowers; meadows, hills and slopes, lowlands as well as mountains up to 1,700 m. Flying period and number of generations depend on altitude. Larva overwinters on various low plants, such as plantain (*Plantago*) and speedwell (*Veronica*).

74 *Melitaea diamina*
False Heath Fritillary
Characteristics: Male and female: Wing length 19–21 mm. Topside of wings very dark with small, pale yellow to yellow-brown spots. Underside of hind wing (no. 74a) pale yellow with orange-brown markings. Each cell of orange-brown submarginal band has small light spot, defined by black mark towards outside. Double marginal lines filled with yellow-brown.

Distribution: North-west Spain, southern and eastern France through central and eastern Europe and central Asia to Amur region. Also Sweden and Norway to approximately 62°N, and south-west Finland. Not western Europe, including British Isles, nor much of southern Europe.

Habitat: Always very local in bogs and damp meadows.

Life History: Single generation on wing June–July. Eggs deposited on plantain (*Plantago*), cow wheat (*Melampyrum*) and various other plants. Half-grown larva over-winters.

75 *Mellicta athalia athalia*
Heath Fritillary
Characteristics: Male: Wing length 18–20 mm. Topside orange-brown with strong, dark markings. Underside of forewing (no. 75a) has irregular, yellow, crescent-shaped marginal spots; crescent in cell 2 has particularly strong black line towards inside; post-discal spots heavily reduced or completely missing. Space between double marginal lines on hind wing matches ground colour. Light underside of abdomen. Female slightly larger and often darker. Subspecies *celadussa* found in south-west Europe and Italy, similar to subspecies *athalia*, but male genitals slightly different.
Distribution: Various subspecies occur throughout Europe; only southern British Isles. Further east through Soviet Union and Asia to Japan.
Habitat and Life History: Woodland meadows, moors and dry areas with poor soil. In British Isles single generation on wing in June; further south, second generation on wing late summer. For larva: see no. 236.

76 *Mellicta deione deione*
Provençal Fritillary
Characteristics: Male: Wing length 16–22 mm. Ground colour lighter orange-brown than no. 75, with more delicate dark markings. Dark marking, shaped like dumb-bell. in middle of back edge of forewing. On underside of fore-wing (no. 76a) is faint dark shadow inside yellow marginal crescent in cell 2. Often reddish spots in each cell of orange sub-marginal band on underside of hind wing. Female has paler top-side and brighter colour contrasts.
Distribution: Spain, Portugal and southern France. Other subspecies in North Africa and western and southern Alps.
Habitat and Life History: Mainly mountain slopes with flowers. Two generations on wing May–June and August–September. The larvae live on species of toadflax (*Linaria*) and snapdragon (*Antirrhinum*).

77 *Mellicta parthenoides*
Meadow Fritillary
Characteristics: Male: Wing length 16–18 mm. Well-defined dark markings on topside, especially round discal spots on forewing. Underside of hind wing pale yellow with orange submarginal band, divided by black lines into crescent-shaped spots. Female often bigger, with grey dust on top-side and broader submarginal band.
Distribution: Spain, Portugal,

France, south-western Bavaria and Switzerland, and western Italy. *Habitat and Life History:* Hilly areas and mountain slopes up to 2,000 m. In lowlands the two generations fly May–June and August–September; but in higher mountain areas the single generation on wing June–August. Larva lives on same plants as larva of no. 76.

78 *Mellicta aurelia*
Nickerl's Fritillary
Characteristics: Male and female: Wing length 14–16 mm. Topside has strong and regular dark markings on orange-brown ground, sometimes covered with dark dust. Underside of the hind wing (no. 78a) has clearly-defined orange-brown submarginal band. Narrow gap between two marginal lines slightly darker than ground. Topside of palps often rusty-red (cf. the following species).
Distribution: North-eastern France, through central and eastern Europe to Caucasus and central Asia.
Habitat and Life History: Damp meadows and bogs. Single generation, on wing June–July. Larva overwinters on plants like plantain (*Plantago*), cow wheat (*Melampyrum*), speedwell (*Veronica*) and others.

Mellicta britomartis
Assman's Fritillary
This eastern species similar to no. 78 (*aurelia*), but somewhat bigger, with slightly darker space between two marginal lines on hind wing. Palps black and yellow, underside of abdomen yellow with two dark stripes. Often on wing with *aurelia* in eastern Europe. Seen as far west as western Germany, also eastern Sweden, in woodland meadows, peat bogs and dry places. Similar biology to no. 78.

79 *Euphydryas maturna*
Scarce Fritillary
Characteristics: Male and female: Wing length 21–25 mm. Topside ground reddish-brown with very strong black-brown markings. Light spots near front margin of forewing and in row outside central cell on hind wing. Underside (no. 79a) has orange-red borders; irregular black submarginal crescents on hind wing.
Distribution and Habitat: Very sporadic. Central and southern Sweden, eastern Finland, Baltic states, northern Germany and in narrow strip from Paris region through Germany to eastern Europe. Prefers open, wild hardwood forests on damp soil near streams.
Life History: Single generation on wing June–July. Excellent flier, will fly very high during mating flight. Visits flowers. Eggs deposited in groups on leaves of ash (*Fraxinus*), beech (*Fagus*), aspen (*Populus tremula*) and honey-

suckle (*Lonicera*). For larva: see no. 237.

80 *Euphydryas iduna*
Lapland Fritillary
Characteristics: Male and female: Wing length 18–19 mm. Cream-coloured topside. Greyish-black markings and reddish-brown spots in central cells and post-discal sections of both wings. Also reddish-brown marginal line. Underside similar to topside, but without greyish-black markings.
Distribution: Scandinavia and Finland north of 64°N, also Caucasus and mountain areas of Asia.
Habitat and Life History: Boggy terrain with scattered tree vegetation and mountain sides up to 700 m. Common locally. Single generation on wing June–July. Details of larva and host plant unknown.

81 *Euphydryas cynthia*
Cynthia's Fritillary
Characteristics: Male: Wing length 19–21 mm. Ground of topside whitish, more or less covered with brownish-black dust. Both wings have reddish-brown post-discal bands of varying width, with small black spot in each cell on hind wing. Underside of hind wing (no. 81a) pale yellow with orange-brown bands and margins. Female (no. 81b) has orange-brown topside with brownish-black markings. Underside similar to no. 81a. Illustrations show sub-species *alpicola* which is darker than the type species *cynthia, cynthia*.
Distribution: Alps in Bavaria, Austria, Switzerland, France and Italy. Also mountains in Bulgaria.
Habitat and Life History: Mountain moors with scrub vegetation from 400 to almost 3,000 m. On wing May to August, depending on altitude. Larvae live socially and overwinter in web on such plants as alp plantain (*Plantago alpina*) and lady's mantle (*Alchemilla*).

82 *Euphydryas aurinia aurinia*
Marsh Fritillary
Characteristics: Male and female: Wing length 17–21 mm. Ground colour of topside yellowish-brown, spots in central cell, and 6 small black spots in post-discal band. Male has faint black marking, female somewhat stronger markings with dark dust. Underside (no. 82a) paler than topside, light orange-brown post-discal band on hind wing has black spots similar to topside. Underside of forewing has no distinct black spots. Subspecies *beckeri* in Iberian Peninsula larger with broader post-discal bands.
Distribution: Most of Europe except Alps; fairly local in Italy. Sweden to about 62°N and southern Finland; some colonies in British Isles, in pest proportions in Ireland. Eastwards through Soviet Union and temperate areas of Asia to Korea.

Habitat and Life History: Favours heather bogs, meadows and dry slopes with flowers. Single generation on wing May–June. Larva lives socially in common web on plants like plantain (*Plantago*), scabious (*Scabiosa*) and others.

83 *Melanargia galathea*
Marbled White

Characteristics: Male: Wing length 23–26 mm. Topside has black and white 'chess-board' markings. Central cell of forewing white at base and black at top with no black cross line or band. Underside (no. 83a) of hind wing whitish with greyish-brown discal and submarginal band. Latter divided by cell 4 with few ocelli, but discal band very narrow at cell 4. Female bigger with ochre-yellow underside and lighter markings.

Distribution: Southern Baltic coastline forms northern limit of range in Europe. Also southern and eastern British Isles. Replaced by *Melanargia lachesis* in south-east France and Spain.

Habitat: Meadows and grass-covered fields.

Life History: Single generation on wing June–July. Eggs deposited during flight. Larva (see no. 238) feeds on grasses.

Melanargia lachesis
Most common of *Melanargia* species in Spain and Portugal, widespread May–June at 900–1,800 m. Also south-east France.

Differs from *galathea* (no. 83) being much lighter particularly at base of hind wing, with whiter central cell on forewing. Discal band on underside of hind wing also narrower near front margin. Unknown in British Isles.

84 *Melanargia russiae*
Esper's Marbled White

Characteristics: Male: Wing length 26–30 mm. Much more delicate dark markings on topside than no. 83. Topside of forewing has zig-zag across middle. Topside of hind wing has large white spot at base and ocelli. Underside (no. 84a) of hind wing has clear, delicate markings and distinct submarginal ocelli. Female has heavier markings and more yellowish ground colour.

Distribution: Widespread in mountain areas in eastern and northern Spain, Portugal and southern France. Subspecies, *japygia*, with darker markings, found in mountain areas in southern Italy and Sicily. Main species also found in southern Soviet Union and south-west Asia.

Habitat and Life History: Local in scattered colonies. In Spain on wing June–July, usually at 1,000–2,000 m, on fairly dry, stony mountain slopes. Larva lives on annual meadow grass (*Poa annua*).

85 *Melanargia occitanica*
Western Marbled White

Characteristics: Male: Wing length

25–28 mm. Two small ocelli on topside of forewing. Broad black cross band on central cell sometimes connected to black area at end of central cell. Topside of hind wing also has ocelli with blue centres. Underside (no. 85a) of hind wing has heavy brown dust along veins and blue-centred ocelli similar to those on topside. White marginal spots, oblong and acute-angled. Female often bigger and underside more heavily covered with dust.

Distribution: Local in Portugal and Spain, except north- and south-west. Also southern France, western Italy, Corsica and Sicily and North Africa.

Habitat and Life History: Mountain slopes up to 1,800 m. On wing April, May or June, depending on altitude. Larva lives on *Lygeum spartum.*

86 *Melanargia arge*
Italian Marbled White

Characteristics: Male and female: Wing length 25–28 mm. Similar to previous species, but more delicate markings on topside, especially cross bar on central cell. Underside (no. 86a) of hind wing has more delicate, but darker, stripes along veins; ocelli more prominent. White marginal spots short and almost right-angled.

Distribution, Habitat and Life History: Mountain areas and hills in central and southern Italy and Sicily. Sporadic colonies from low-

lands to approximately 2,500 m. On wing May and early June. Host plant of larva unknown.

87 *Melanargia ines*
Spanish Marbled White

Characteristics: Male: Wing length 23–25 mm. Distinguishable from nos. 85 and 86 by broad, isolated, black cross bar in central cell, by very big, prominent ocelli (no. 87a) and flat, crescent-shaped marginal spots on underside of hind wings and by absence of curved line in cell 1b. Short, dark cross lines at front margin of hind wing. Female larger with yellower ground.

Distribution, Habitat and Life History: Very similar to no. 85, but confined to Spain and Portugal, except north west. Host plant not known.

88 *Hipparchia fagi*
Woodland Grayling

Characteristics: Male and female: Wing length 33–40 mm. Topside brownish-black, pale yellow post-discal band with ocelli in cells 2 and 5 on forewing, while hind wing has whiter post-discal band, clearest on female, also small ocellus in cell 2. Inner edge of light band on hind wing almost straight. Underside of forewing similar to topside, but band more distinctly marked. Underside of hind wing predominantly brownish-black with light markings, post-discal band lightly speckled with dark scales. Extent of light band varies.

Distribution: France and north-east Spain through central and southern Europe to southern Soviet Union. Northern limit about 52°N, in central Germany.

Habitat and Life History: Only local within distribution area. Likes open, light hardwood forests and scrub, below 1,000 m. On wing July–August. Butterfly often sits on tree trunks with wings folded. Larva lives on various *Holcus* species, notably velvet grass. Overwinters and fully grown by May. Pupa lies freely on ground.

89 *Hipparchia alcyone*
Rock Grayling

Characteristics: Male and female: Wing length 27–36 mm. Very similar to previous species, although considerably smaller. Bands on topside yellower, band on male forewing more pronounced, while inner edge of light band on hind wing clearly curved in the middle. Extent of light bands varies.

Distribution: Widespread in Iberian Peninsula. Western limit southern and eastern France and western Germany to Baltic coast. Found through central, southern and eastern Europe to Caucasus and Kurdistan. Fairly rare in mainland Italy and unknown in Po valley. Remarkable, isolated population in south-east Norway.

Habitat and Life History: Usually

not as local as no. 88, and less frequent in north part of range. In southern Europe is mainly mountain species, on stony slopes, in Alps to about 1,400 m, in Spain to 2,000 m and above. In dry, sandy places in lowlands. On wing June–August. Larva overwinters on false brome grass (*Brachypodium*).

90 *Hipparchia neomiris*
Corsican Grayling

Characteristics: Male: Wing length 23–25 mm. Topside brownish-black with orange-yellow post-discal bands on both wings. White band on underside of hind wing, pronounced towards inside, blurred towards outside. Female has lighter ground.

Distribution, Habitat and Life History: Corsica, Sardinia and Elba, on dry mountain slopes 900–2,000 m. On wing June–July.

91 *Hipparchia semele*
Grayling

Characteristics: Male: Wing length 21–25 mm. Dark brown topside with big scent scale below centre of forewing. Both wings have more or less distinct yellow-brown post-discal bands, divided by veins. Ocelli in cells 2 and 5 of forewing, in cell 2 of hind wing. Underside of hind wing (no. 91a) marbled brown, light and dark grey, darkest at base. Female (no. 91b) bigger with distinct yellow-brown bands and bigger ocelli.

Distribution: Most of Europe, Scandinavia as far as 62°N, along southern and south-western coasts of Finland, and chiefly south British Isles. Found through Soviet Union to Armenia.

Habitat: Near coast and uncultivated, sandy inland areas. Prefers warm, dry areas. Up to 1,500 m in Alps.

Life History: Single generation on wing July–August with rapid and vigorous flight. Often sits on sand with folded wings, wonderfully protected by camouflage of hind wings. Male displays to female before mating. Eggs deposited singly on grasses, notably hair grass (*Aira*) and fescue grass (*Festuca*). For larva: see no. 239.

92 *Hipparchia aristaeus*
Southern Grayling

Characteristics: Very similar to no. 91, but colour varies. Orange-brown bands on topside often more extensive than on *semele*, but male genitals only certain distinguishing feature.

Distribution, Habitat and Life History: Mediterranean islands, notably Corsica, Sardinia and Sicily, in southern Italy and Greece on dry, heath-like stretches in mountain areas. On wing June–July. Host plants of larva not known.

93 *Hipparchia statilinus*
Tree Grayling

Characteristics: Male: Wing length 22–23 mm. Topside very dark, greyish-brown to brownish-black, darkest on forewing, with its 2 blind ocelli in cells 2 and 5, and 2 small, white spots in cells 3 and 4. Underside of hind wing (no. 93a) has light greyish-brown basal section, while discal section defined by dark, wavy lines. Further out hind wing is darker brown and grey. Female has clear ocelli, usually with white pupils, obscure, yellow spots in post-discal section on topside of forewing. Extremely variable.

Distribution and Habitat: Southern, western and central Europe as far north as southern Baltic coast; through eastern Europe and Soviet Union to Asia Minor. Frequents heaths and sandy places, often with scattered tree and scrub vegetation. Population generally dwindling.

Life History: Single generation each year on wing July–October. Larva overwinters and lives on grasses, notably sheep fescue (*Festuca ovina*), hair grass (*Aira*) species and barren brome grass (*Bromus sterilis*).

94 *Pseudotergumia fidia*
Striped Grayling

Characteristics: Male: Wing length 28–31 mm. Markings on topside similar to *statilinus* (93). Underside of hind wing variegated whitish-grey and brown with clearly defined dark zig-zags. Female larger with small light post-discal spots near front and back margins.

Distribution, Habitat and Life History: Spain and Portugal, except north west, southern France and Italian Maritime Alps, also North Africa. Frequents mountain slopes with sparse tree vegetation, on wing July–August. Larva lives on various grasses.

95 *Chazara briseis*
Hermit

Characteristics: Male: Wing length 20–21 mm, size variable (see figs. 95 and 95a). Topside dark brown, both wings have cream-coloured band, divided by dark veins on forewing. Light border on forewing. Underside of hind wing (no. 95a) has two brownish spots outside basal section, marginal section greyer-brown than section inside brown post-discal band. Female larger with less distinct bands on topside and less clear markings on underside.

Distribution: Southern and central Europe up to central Germany at 50°N. On some Mediterranean islands and eastwards to western Asia.

Habitat and Life History: Locally in dry, stony places, often on mountain slopes; in Spain to over 2,000 m. In lowlands butterfly on wing in May, later at higher altitudes. Larva overwinters September–June on purple moor grass (*Molinia coerulea*) and other grasses. Pupa lies in top soil under grass roots.

96 *Oeneis bore*
Arctic Grayling

Characteristics: Male and female: Wing length 22–25 mm. Topside greyish-yellow without distinct markings, post-discal section often slightly paler yellow. Underside of hind wing brown and lightly marbled with more or less distinct whitish rim outside discal band. Often rather worn.

Distribution: Confined to northernmost Scandinavia and Finland between 67°N and 70°N; also northern Soviet Union.

Habitat and Life History: Dry heaths in mountains and sandy coasts. Mainly on wing in July, only in good weather. Larva lives on grasses, notably sheep fescue (*Festuca ovina*) and overwinters twice. Pupa lies on ground between grass roots.

97 *Oeneis norna*
Norse Grayling

Characteristics: Male: Wing length 26–28 mm. Pale brown topside with broad yellowish post-discal bands. Black spots in cells 2 and 5 of forewing, and often in cell 2 of hind wing. Underside of hind wing (no. 97a) has dark-brown discal band, outside edged with white. Female often lighter with white pupils in ocelli.

Distribution: Scandinavia and Finland north of 62°N. Only in mountains in southern part of range; down to coasts in north where it is most abundant.

Also parts of Asia and North America.

Habitat and Life History: Near bogs and other marshy places, mainly on surrounding sunny slopes with little or no tree vegetation. Single generation on wing July. Larva lives on grasses.

98 *Oeneis glacialis*
Alpine Grayling

Characteristics: Male: Wing length 25–28 mm. Very similar to no. 97, but paler, with less distinct bands; two ocelli on hind wing. Underside of hind wing (no. 98a) has characteristically prominent white veins on dark brown mottled ground. Female bigger and paler.

Distribution, Habitat and Life History: Confined to Alps on slopes with sparse grass vegetation at 2,000–3,000 m. On wing late June–August. Abundant only alternate years in some areas. Presumably larva, which lives on grasses, takes two years to develop.

99 *Oeneis jutta*
Baltic Grayling

Characteristics: Male: Wing length 27–28 mm. Distinct scent-scale spot on topside. Colour variable, yellowish post-discal bands divided into patches enclosing ocelli, sometimes missing from hind wing. Underside of hind wing marbled grey and dark brown. Female (no. 99a) often considerably larger, with more continuous yellow spots

on topside, larger and more constant ocelli.

Distribution: Scandinavia and Finland, Baltic states through northern Soviet Union and Siberia to North America. Confined to Oslo vicinity in Norway, and absent from North Cape and mountains in Sweden and north-east Finland.

Habitat and Life History: Lowlands especially in scattered conifer vegetation round peat bogs and lakes. Male frequents tree trunks, while female prefers low vegetation. On wing May–July, and more abundant alternate years, indicating two-year development. Larva probably lives on grasses.

100 *Satyrus actaea*
Black Satyr

Characteristics: Male: Wing length 24–28 mm. Single ocellus with white pupil usual on topside of forewing, also erect scent scales in cells 1–3. Underside of hind wing (no. 100a) usually has distinct greyish-white band defining outside of dark brown basal section. Female larger with lighter brown ground colour, and two ocelli with white pupils, occasionally surrounded by pale yellow rings on topside of forewing. Species varies.

Distribution: Iberian Peninsula and French Mediterranean coast to Maritime Alps in west Italy. Also Asia Minor, Syria and Iran.

Habitat and Life History: In Europe locally on dry mountain slopes with sparse vegetation from 900–

2,000 m. On wing June–August. Larva lives on various grasses.

101 *Satyrus ferula*
Sooty Satyr
Characteristics: Male: Wing length 25–30 mm. Topside of forewing has two ocelli with white pupils in cells 2 and 5, and occasional white spots in cells 3 and 4. Underside of hind wing (no. 101a) has paler rim outside basal section. Female (no. 101b) is bigger, much lighter brown with ocelli on topside on orange-brown ground. Underside of forewing predominantly orange-yellow with large ocelli. Underside of hind wing lighter than male.
Distribution: Southern and central France through southern Alps to Balkans; also Apennines. Northern limit about 40°N. Not Iberian Peninsula, but Morocco and parts of south-west Asia.
Habitat and Life History: Like no. 100 on mountain slopes from 500–1,500 m, where it prefers stony, sunny places with sparse grass vegetation. On wing June–August. Larva lives on various grasses, especially *Aira caespitosa*.

102 *Minois dryas*
Dryad
Characteristics: Male: Wing length 27–29 mm. Similar to no. 101, but ocelli on topside have blue pupils; hind wing margin scalloped. Female often considerably bigger than male, lighter brown with larger ocelli.

Distribution: France through central Europe, northern Italy, eastern Europe and southern Soviet Union to central Asia and Japan. Confined to few places in northern Spain. In Germany absent from north-west but on Baltic in few places.
Habitat and Life History: Local in most parts of range and up to 1,500 m in Alps. On wing June–September. Frequents meadows and grass-covered slopes with scattered tree vegetation. Larva overwinters on various grasses.

103 *Arethusana arethusa*
False Grayling
Characteristics: Male: Wing length 22–24 mm. Prominent scent-scale spot on forewing. Orange band of disconnected spots, often very reduced, on topside. Blind ocellus in cell 5. Big orange section on underside of forewing. Hind wing brownish with lighter band outside basal section. Female (no. 103a) bigger with more prominent orange band.
Distribution: Iberian Peninsula and France north of Alps to Balkans. Also widespread in northern Italy. Eastwards through Asia Minor and southern Soviet Union to central Asia.
Habitat and Life History: Local in dry, stony places with calcareous soil. On wing July–August. Larva lives on various grasses, especially fescue (*Festuca*) species. Pupa lies on ground.

104 *Brintesia circe*
Banded Grayling
Characteristics: Male and female: Wing length 33–40 mm. Broad, white band divided by veins on topside. Blind ocellus on forewing. On underside similar white band, outside which wing is mottled brown and white.
Distribution: Southern and central Europe as far north as central Germany. Eastwards through Asia Minor to Iran and Himalayas.
Habitat and Life History: Open woods; often sits on tree trunks. On wing June–August. Larva overwinters on various grasses, notably rye grass (*Lolium*) and brome grass (*Bromus*).

EREBIA

Erebia is a big Satyridae genus, sometimes extremely difficult to identify, with over 40 species in Europe; many species have several subspecies so there are very many named forms. Most *Erebia* species are found in mountain areas in central and southern Europe with very small ranges. The first group mentioned below (nos. 105–106) comprises two species confined to Scandinavia and Finland, the next five species (nos. 107–111) have wider range in central Europe; nos. 107–109 are also found in Scandinavia and Finland. Others are central and southern European species with more or less limited distribution. Only two species, *aethiops* (no. 111) and *epiphron* (no. 113) are found in British Isles. *Ligea* (no. 109) is very occasionally found in Denmark. *Medusa* (no. 108) and *aethiops* (no. 111) are the only *Erebia* species found in north Germany and Holland.

105 *Erebia embla*
Lapland Ringlet
Characteristics: Male and female: Wing length 25–26 mm. Topside has two merging apical ocelli with or without white pupils and further ocelli in cells 2 and 3, sometimes in cell 1b. Topside of hind wing has 3 or 4 ocelli, all with yellowish-brown edges. Female has lighter brown ground colour than male, and more yellowish-brown round ocelli.
Distribution: Confined to Scandinavia and Finland, and northern Soviet Union and Asia.
Habitat and Life History: Locally in wet bogs with scrub vegetation surrounded by coniferous forest; mainly at heights of a few hundred

metres. On wing mainly June–July. Larva probably lives on grasses, details uncertain.

106 *Erebia disa*
Arctic Ringlet
Characteristics: Male and female: Wing length 23–25 mm. Topside similar to no. 105, but hind wing lacks ocelli, and apical ocelli on forewing smaller and more detached. Female has lighter brown topside than male.
Distribution: Northern Scandinavia and Finland; southern limit round Gulf of Bothnia. Also northern Soviet Union, northern Siberia and North America.
Habitat and Life History: Very wet meadows and bogs, often in partly-flooded places. Mainly at fairly low altitudes. On wing June–July. Little known about life history.

107 *Erebia pandrosa*
Dewy Ringlet
Characteristics: Male: Wing length 20–25 mm. In cells 2–5 on topside of forewing is broad, reddish-brown post-discal band, defined towards inside by dark line with black spot in each cell. Dark transverse line in central cell. Hind wing often has black, red-ringed spots. Underside of hind wing (no. 107a) is silvery with irregular dark lines on both sides of discal band. Female often lighter without post-discal spots on forewing.
Distribution: Eastern Pyrenees and

Alps; western Scandinavian peninsula and northern Finland. Also mountain areas in eastern Europe, Balkans and central Asia.
Habitat and Life History: In Pyrenees and Alps between 1,600 and 3,000 m, in southern Norway to 900 m, but lower further north. Found in mountain areas with short grass vegetation. On wing June–August; but only on wing during a period of 3 weeks in each locality. Larva overwinters on fescue (*Festuca*) species.

108 *Erebia medusa*
Woodland Ringlet
Characteristics: Male: Wing length 21–24 mm. On topside of forewing ocelli with white pupils in cells 2, 4 and 5, all ringed with yellowish-brown band interrupted in cell 3. Sometimes additional small ocelli in cells 1b and 6. Topside of hind wing has 3–4 ocelli. Underside (no. 108a) of hind wing almost uniformly brown, with ocelli similar to topside. Female has paler ground with broader and brighter yellow rings round ocelli. Fringes of uniform colour; antennae brown.
Distribution: Central France through central and eastern Europe to Balkans and Asia Minor. Also Baltic in Poland. Subspecies, *polaris*, in Scandinavia and north-west Germany.
Habitat and Life History: Meadows and bogs, often surrounded by forests; various forms lowlands to

2,600 m in Alps. The arctic sub-species *polaris* in mountain meadows north of 68°N. For larva: see no. 240.

109 *Erebia ligea*
Arran Brown
Characteristics: Male: Wing length 24–27 mm. Both fore- and hind wings have broad reddish-brown bands, former enclosing 3–4 ocelli, latter enclosing 3 ocelli, with or without white pupils. Underside (no. 109a) of hind wing has ocelli and white line from front edge. Female has lighter ground, paler orange-red bands on topside, and indistinct light post-discal band on underside of hind wing. Both sexes have chequered fringes.
Distribution: Scandinavia and Finland, central and eastern Europe as far north as 51°N and west to the Jura and Vosges in eastern France; also Auvergne and Apennines. Through Asia to Japan.
Habitat and Life History: Evenly distributed in all Nordic countries, though northern species smaller, darker with less clear markings. Found in meadows surrounded by forests, especially hardwood forests. On wing from late June–August. Tiny larva overwinters and lives on forest grasses, notably millet grass (*Milium effusus*) and Polish millet (*Digitaria sanguinalis*). Most larvae overwinter twice and pupate when nearly two years old.

110 *Erebia euryale*
Large Ringlet
Characteristics: Male: Wing length 21–23 mm. Very similar to no. 109 with variable markings. Noticeably smaller than *ligea* (no. 109), with smaller, rounder ocelli often without white pupils. Underside of hind wing reddish-brown with 3–4 ocelli with red rings and white pupils. Female paler ground colour, with more yellowish-red bands on topside, often light dust in band round ocelli.
Distribution: Several subspecies in mountain areas in southern, central and eastern Europe, including Balkans; also in Alps and Pyrenees. Northernmost occurrence in south German mountain areas and Sudeten Mountains. Also Ural and Altai Mountains.
Habitat and Life History: Coniferous forest zone; in mountain areas from 1,100 m to timber line around 2,000 m. On wing July and early August. Larva lives on same grasses as no. 109; development probably takes two years.

111 *Erebia aethiops*
Scotch Argus
Characteristics: Male: Wing length 22–26 mm. On topside of forewing reddish-brown post-discal band narrow in middle around cell 3 with 3 white-pupilled ocelli. Topside of hind wing has 3–4 small, white-pupilled ocelli on reddish-brown ground, while underside (no. 111a) is brown

with lighter post-discal bands enclosing 3–4 tiny white spots. Female lighter brown ground colour, yellowish-brown post-discal bands, and yellowish-brown underside of hind wing with darker discal bands.

Distribution: Belgium and north-east France through central and eastern Europe to Asia Minor, Urals and Caucasus. Reaches south-eastern coast of Baltic, also northern British Isles. South of Alps only in mountain areas of north-west Italy.

Habitat and Life History: Woodland meadows and light, open woods with conifers. Up to about 1,800 m. On wing July till late September, depending on altitude. Larva lives on various grasses.

112 *Erebia epistygne*
Spring Ringlet

Characteristics: Male and female: Wing length 22–25 mm. Easily recognised by light spot in central cell of forewing and by broad, yellow post-discal band with three merging ocelli near front. Topside of hind wing has 4–5 red-ringed ocelli. Underside of hind wing has dark discal band, while basal and post-discal sections mottled pale greyish-brown to yellowish-grey, slightly paler on female, with her yellowish-brown lines along veins.

Distribution: South-eastern France, central and north-eastern Spain.

Habitat and Life History: Hilly and mountainous terrain with sparse tree vegetation; in mountains of Spain up to 2,000 m and over, lower in south-east France. On wing once snow has melted, from March–April to May–June. Host plants of larva not known, probably grass species.

113 *Erebia epiphron*
Mountain Ringlet

Characteristics: Male: Wing length 17–20 mm. Topside of forewing has more or less distinct reddish-brown band usually enclosing 4 black spots with or without white pupils. Topside of hind wing has similar band with 3 black spots. Underside (no. 113a) of hind wing brown with 2–3 ocelli, sometimes none. Female usually has bigger, black spots, often with white pupils.

Distribution: European mountain areas, such as Sudeten Mountains, Vosges, Bavaria, Alps, Auvergne, Pyrenees, Apennines and Cantabrian Mountains. Found locally in British Isles, Scotland and Westmorland. Absent from Scandinavia and Finland.

Habitat and Life History: Grassy slopes with rich flower vegetation, mainly 1,200–2,000 m. On wing late June to August. Larva overwinters on various grasses. Pupates May–June; pupal stage lasts a couple of weeks.

114 *Erebia pharte*
Blind Ringlet
Characteristics: Male: Wing length
17–20 mm. Topside of forewing
has reddish-yellow band of uniform, rectangular spots. Topside
of hind wing has similar, but
smaller, row of spots. Underside
(no. 114a) has similar bands. No
black spots on topside or underside. Female lighter, with particularly extensive yellow dusting
on underside (no. 114a).
*Distribution, Habitat and Life His-
tory:* Only Alps and Tatra Mountains, from 1,200–2,500 m. Mountain meadows straddling timber
line. On wing July–August. Host
plants of larva not known.

115 *Erebia gorge gorge*
Silky Ringlet
Characteristics: Male: Wing length
17–20 mm. Several well-defined
subspecies with considerable variations. Topside of forewing has
broad, silky, red band, enclosing
2 or 3 apical ocelli with white
pupils. Sometimes further ocelli
in cells 2 and 3. Top- and underside of hind wing of subspecies
gorge (no. 115) have no ocelli, but
subspecies *ramondi* (no. 115a) has
4 ocelli with white pupils. Underside mottled light and dark greyish-
brown. Female paler than male.
Distribution: European mountain
areas, notably Alps, Apennines,
Pyrenees and Cantabrian Mountains. Also eastern European
mountain areas and Balkans.

Habitat and Life History: Frequent
in suitable habitats, such as
exposed new moraines and fallen
rocks, with little or no vegetation.
Found at 1,500–3,000 m from
June till August. Larva lives on
grasses.

116 *Erebia cassioides*
Brassy Ringlet
Characteristics: Male: Wing length
16–18 mm. Topside of forewing
has short yellowish-brown band
enclosing 2 ocelli with white
pupils. Topside of hind wing has
3 ocelli with white pupils surrounded by yellowish-brown.
Underside of hind wing grey,
often with two dark, narrow
transverse lines defining discal
band. Female has lighter markings. Species represents group of 6
European species (*tyndarus* group),
all very similar, but with some
variations. Genetic research has
shown that only a single species
occurs in any given locality. Distribution pattern forms very compli-
cated mosaic, as various species
often only separated by altitude.
Distribution: Mountain areas from
Cantabrian Mountains and Pyrenees in west through Alps and
mountains of mainland Italy to
mountain areas in Balkans.
Habitat and Life History: Like other
species of *tyndarus* group, *cassioides*
found on grass-covered slopes.
On wing late June to late August
at 1,650–1,800 m. Larva lives on
grasses.

117 *Erebia neoridas*
Autumn Ringlet
Characteristics: Male and female: Wing length 20–23 mm. Remarkable broad wings. Yellowish-red band on topside of forewing narrows towards back, enclosing two merging ocelli near front and smaller ocellus near back. Topside of hind wing has ocelli surrounded by yellowish-brown in cells 2–4. Underside of hind wing dark brown with greyish-brown postdiscal band.
Distribution: From eastern Pyrenees through southern France to northwest Italy. Also mountain areas in central Italy.
Habitat and Life History: Hilly and mountainous terrain at 600–1,500 m. On wing August–September. Food plants of larva unknown.

118 *Erebia pronoe*
Water Ringlet
Characteristics: Male: Wing length 21–25 mm. Topside of forewing varies from brownish-black with faint ocelli in indistinct band (as illustrated) to brownish-black with 3–5 mm wide reddish-brown band enclosing two apical ocelli and one ocellus in cell 2. Topside of hind wing may have no ocelli or 2–3. Underside (no. 118a) of hind wing has dark brown discal band, rest violet-grey owing to scattered silver-grey dust. Female is paler on both sides.
Distribution: Alps, Pyrenees and mountain areas in eastern Europe and Balkans.
Habitat and Life History: Grass-covered mountain slopes often surrounded by forests, especially at 1,000–1,500 m, occasionally higher. On wing mid-July–late September. Larva overwinters on grasses, especially meadow grass (*Poa*).

119 *Erebia oeme*
Bright-eyed Ringlet
Characteristics: Male: Wing length 19–22 mm. Reddish-brown band does not contrast clearly with ground colour. On forewing two ocelli with white pupils and smaller ocellus in cell 2; hind wing has three white-pupilled, red-ringed ocelli. Underside very similar to topside, but ocelli often bigger. Some forms have reduced ocelli. Female paler with bigger ocelli, and 6 ocelli of various sizes on underside of hind wing (no. 119a). Easily confused with no. 108, but antennae black-tipped.
Distribution: Mountain areas in Europe, from Pyrenees across Jura and northern Alps to Carpathians in eastern Europe.
Habitat and Life History: Prefers damp meadows, particularly at 900–1,800 m. On wing June–July. Larva overwinters on woodrush (*Luzula*) species.

120 *Maniola jurtina*
Meadow Brown
Characteristics: Male: Wing length

22–25 mm. Topside greyish-brown with broad scent-scale spot under central cell. Also black, with white pupil inside tip of wing. Occasional obscure orange area behind ocellus. Underside of forewing predominantly pale orange. Underside of hind wing greyish- to yellowish-brown, discal section darkest; two small, black post-discal spots in cells 2 and 5. Female (no. 120a) bigger with orange-yellow markings on topside of forewing. Underside of hind wing has clear band without male's black spots.

Distribution: Most of Europe, except Scandinavia and Finland north of 62°N. Eastwards to Urals, Asia Minor and Iran. Very common and widespread in British Isles.

Habitat: Meadows and grassy fields; up to about 1,800 m.

Life History: Long flying period from June to early September, but particularly July. On wing even in cloudy weather. Eggs, ½ mm in diameter, deposited singly on grasses, especially annual meadow grass (*Poa annua*). For larva: see no. 241.

121 *Hyponephele lycaon*
Dusky Meadow Brown

Characteristics: Male: Wing length 20–24 mm. Very similar to no. 120, but scent-scale spot on forewing smaller and more forward-curved. More or less distinct yellowish-brown tint on post-

discal section on topside of fore-wing. Underside of forewing mainly yellowish-brown with white-pupilled apical ocellus and brown marginal band. Underside of hind wing greyish-brown, almost without markings or with slightly darker discal band. Ground colour of female (no. 121a) variable, forewing has orange-yellow post-discal band enclosing one or two black spots. Topside of hind wing has indistinct, paler post-discal band.

Distribution: Iberian Peninsula through southern France, southern and central Europe to Caucasus and central Asia. Southern coast of Baltic.

Habitat and Life History: Dry, sandy and stony places, such as forest clearings. Chiefly lowland species. Species has declined during last couple of decades and occurs locally. Butterfly visits thistle flowers. Single generation each year. Larva overwinters on various grasses, notably annual meadow grass (*Poa annua*).

Hyponephele lupina
Oriental Meadow Brown

Hyponephele lupina found in central and southern Spain, Portugal, south-eastern France and Apennines. Larger than *lycaon* (no. 121), male has broader scent-scale stripe and lacks light-brown scales on topside. Margin of hind wing more deeply scalloped in both sexes.

122 *Aphantopus hyperantus*
Ringlet
Characteristics: Male: Wing length 20–24 mm. Topside brownish-black with variable number of obscure ocelli. Underside (no. 122a) lighter brown with distinct yellow-ringed, white-pupilled ocelli. Female lighter brown with larger, more regular ocelli.
Distribution: Most of Europe, except Scandinavia and Finland north of 64°N. Common in British Isles and found in northern Iberian Peninsula, but not Italy. Eastwards to Pacific coast.
Habitat and Life History: Damp, grass-covered places, often with scattered trees, from lowlands to 1,500 m. Single generation on wing late June–late August. Visits flowers, especially of blackberry. Female deposits eggs during flight. Tiny larva overwinters, fully grown in June. Lives on grasses, such as *Poa* and *Milium*. Pupal stage lasts couple of weeks.

123 *Pyronia tithonus*
Gatekeeper
Characteristics: Male: Wing length 17–19 mm. Topside of forewing has large, pointed scent-scale spot. Basal section has no dark dust. Orange markings on topside of hind wing vary in size, occasional ocellus in cell 2. Underside of hind wing (no. 123a) yellowish-brown with reddish tint, basal section blurred yellow; small, ocelli with white pupils in cells 2 and 5.

Female (no. 123b) bigger, lacking scent-scale spot, more orange-yellow on topside, with yellower underside.
Distribution: Locally, British Isles, France, Spain and Portugal east through central and southern Europe to Asia Minor and Caucasus. Parts of Alps and southern Italy.
Habitat and Life History: Chiefly lowland, in open woods, along edges of woods and in scrub, especially blackberry. To 900 m in mountains. On wing July–August. Eggs deposited singly on food plants of larva, notably, annual meadow grass (*Poa annua*) and *Milium* species. Tiny larva overwinters. Pupa sits on grass straw and takes 3 weeks to develop. Males hatch before females.

124 *Pyronia cecilia*
Southern Gatekeeper
Characteristics: Male: Wing length 15–16 mm. Similar to no. 123. Scent-scale spot on topside rectangular and crossed with yellow veins. Topside of hind wing has no ocelli, neither has underside of hind wing (no. 124a). Female (no. 124b) bigger, without scent-scale spot; markings on underside often clearer.
Distribution: Iberian Peninsula except north, south-east France, mainland Italy, Mediterranean islands and parts of Balkans. Not north of southern alpine valleys in Switzerland nor South Tyrol.

Also Asia Minor and North Africa. *Habitat and Life History:* Like nos. 122 and 123 frequents open, warm places in uncultivated terrain, preferably with sparse scrub vegetation. On wing June–August. Larva overwinters on grasses, especially *Aira caespitosa.*

125 *Pyronia bathseba*
Spanish Gatekeeper
Characteristics: Male: Wing length 18–19 mm. Forewing darker than nos. 123 and 124, as basal section covered with dark brown dust enclosing scent-scale spot. Reddish-yellow band encloses couple of black ocelli with white pupils. Hind wing has similar band, enclosing three small ocelli. Underside (no. 125a) of hind wing has distinct, yellow discal band and 5 obscure, light-ringed ocelli. Female (no. 125b) bigger with lighter topside on forewing.
Distribution: Iberian Peninsula, except north-west, and south-east France. Different subspecies found in North Africa.
Habitat and Life History: Abundant in Spain and Portugal up to about 1,800 m. On wing April through summer. Larva feeds on various grasses.

126 *Coenonympha tullia*
Large Heath
Characteristics: Male: Wing length 19–20 mm. Topside of forewing almost plain, greyish-brown with orange tint, at times paler than

illustrated, with small, obscure yellow-ringed ocellus, marginal section no darker than rest. Topside of hind wing with or without 2–3 yellow-ringed ocelli. Underside (no. 126a) has greyish hind wing with irregular, light postdiscal band and 5–6 small, black, white-pupilled and light-ringed ocelli. Some of ocelli very small. Female (no. 126b) has lighter topside. Species very variable; forms with more distinct ocelli found in other parts of Europe.
Distribution: Scandinavia and Finland (except north-west), northern British Isles, Belgium, northeast France and Germany and east through temperate areas of Asia to Pacific. Also North America.
Habitat: Damp, grassy meadows, swamps and bogs.
Life History: On wing, rather heavy and sluggish, June–July. Does not normally visit flowers. Eggs deposited singly on cotton grass (*Eriophorum*) and white beak rush (*Rhynchospora alba*). Half-grown larva overwinters at roots of grass straw October till April–May, when it resumes eating and becomes fully grown. Pupal stage lasts 3–4 weeks.

127 *Coenonympha pamphilus*
Small Heath
Characteristics: Male and female: Wing length 14–17 mm. Topside reddish-yellow with narrow grey marginal border on both pairs of

wings. Underside (no. 127a) of hind wing has fairly dark basal section near front. Rest light greyish-brown with few obscure ocelli. Underside of forewing has distinct ocellus.

Distribution: Throughout Europe and eastwards to central and south-west Asia. Absent from northernmost Scandinavia and Finland. Also North Africa. Very common in British Isles.

Habitat: Open, grassy places up to 1,800 m.

Life History: Two generations in northern Europe on wing May–September. More generations and longer flying period further south. On wing in cloudy weather, if warm enough. Eggs deposited on grasses, notably annual meadow grass (*Poa annua*). For larva: see no. 242.

128 *Coenonympha dorus*
Dusky Heath

Characteristics: Male: Wing length 16–17 mm. Topside of forewing dark brownish-grey with big, yellow-ringed, blind ocellus near tip and smaller ocellus near back. Front part of hind wing also greyish-brown, back orange-yellow with several blind ocelli forming curve in cells 1–4. Occasional small ocellus in cell 6. Underside (no. 128a) has double, dark marginal line. Forewing very light with large, white-pupilled ocellus. Hind wing greyish-yellow near base, post-discal band broad

and light enclosing ocelli similar to those on topside. Female much paler on topside.

Distribution: Iberian Peninsula, south-east France, north-west Italy and mountains in central Italy. Also North Africa.

Habitat and Life History: Dry, warm localities with uncultivated, preferably stony, terrain. Single generation on wing at about 900–1,500 m June–July. Larva feeds on various grasses, such as sheep fescue (*Festuca ovina*).

129 *Coenonympha arcania*
Pearly Heath

Characteristics: Male and female: Wing length 17–20 mm. Distinguished by orange-yellow topside of forewing, with its broad, dark brownish marginal border. Topside of hind wing greyish-brown. Underside (no. 129a) of hind wing has distinct, irregular, whitish post-discal band and black, white-pupilled ocelli in cells 3–4, occasionally also cells 1, 4 and 5. Ocellus outside post-discal band in cell 6.

Distribution: Central and northern Spain through western, central and southern Europe, Asia Minor and southern Soviet Union to Urals.

Habitat: Mainly meadows and grassy slopes in woods and scrub, at 1,200–1,800 m.

Life History: Single generation on wing June–July. More males in evidence than females which hatch a week later. Females possibly less forthcoming. Larva lives on grasses, especially melic grass (*Melica*), fully grown by May.

130 *Coenonympha hero*
Scarce Heath

Characteristics: Male and female: Wing length 15–18 mm. Topside uniformly dark brown with few yellow-ringed ocelli on hind wing. Underside (no. 130a) predominantly grey-brown. On hind wing narrow, irregularly shaped, whitish post discal band. Area outside brownish-orange with row of 6 white-pupilled ocelli. Metallic line between these and dark marginal line.

Distribution: From north-east France, Belgium and southern Holland through central and eastern Germany, Poland and central Soviet Union to Korea and Japan. Also in central and southern Scandinavia and Finland.

Habitat and Life History: Woods with open, variable terrain. Single generation on wing late May to late June. Males emerge week before females. Larva overwinters on grasses.

131 *Coenonympha glycerion*
Chestnut Heath

Characteristics: Male: Wing length 16–18 mm. Topside dark, usually without markings, forewing various tones of chestnut-brown. Underside (no. 131a) of forewing greyish yellow-brown with grey

margin. Underside of hind wing greyish-brown with distinct, white post-discal spots and row of about 6 white-pupilled ocelli. Female has orange-brown forewing topside, but dark grey topside of hind wing sometimes with 2–3 small ocelli.

Distribution: Southern Finland, eastern Europe with isolated populations in Massif Central, eastern Pyrenees, northern and central Spain (the subspecies *iphioides*) and eastwards through Soviet Union to Siberia.

Habitat and Life History: Damp meadows in woodland areas. Up to 1,400 m in Alps. Single generation on wing June–July. Females less mobile. Larva overwinters on various grasses.

132 *Coenonympha oedippus*
False Ringlet

Characteristics: Can be confused with no. 122. Male: Wing length 17–21 mm. Topside (no. 132a) greyish-brown, both fore- and hind wings have big ocelli, one displaced inwards in cell 6 on hind wing. Narrow, metallic line between wing margin and ocelli. Female larger with larger ocelli.

Distribution, Habitat and Life History: South-west France, northern Italy and southernmost central Europe east through Soviet Union and central Asia to Japan. Very sporadic and extinct in southern parts of central Germany. Favours swampy meadows, a rapidly disappearing habitat. Also frequents open woods and scrub. The single annual generation on wing June–July. Larva feeds on sedges (*Carex*) species and iris.

133 *Pararge aegeria aegeria*
Speckled Wood
Characteristics: Male and female: Wing length 19–22 mm. Ground of topside orange-yellow (no. 133) to yellowish-white (no. 133a), palest in populations of central and northern Europe (subspecies *tircis*). Ground colour broken by dark brown criss-crosses. Male has big scent-scale spot below central cell. Margin of hind wing scalloped. Topside of forewing has ocellus just inside tip, topside of hind wing has 3–4 ocelli. Underside of forewing similar to topside. Underside of hind wing greenish with more confused markings.
Distribution: Most of Europe, subspecies *tircis* north of line from Brittany to Po valley, subspecies *aegeria* to south. Northern limit about 62°N. Also eastwards through Soviet Union to central Asia.
Habitat and Life History: Frequents forests. Single generation in central Scandinavia on wing June–July. In Denmark two generations on wing May–June and August; further south more generations on wing from March to October. Eggs deposited singly on several common grasses. Pupa overwinters.

134 *Lasiommata megera*
Wall Brown
Characteristics: Male: Wing length 19–25 mm. Ground of topside light yellowish-brown with dark brown criss-crosses. Big scent scale spot and large ocellus on forewing. Hind wing has 3–4 smaller ocelli. Underside of hind wing light greyish-brown with delicate dark markings and 6 brown-ringed ocelli. Female (no. 134a) often larger and paler.
Distribution: Southern and central Europe to approximately 60°N. Also North Africa. Eastwards to Syria, Iran and Soviet Union.
Habitat and Life History: Open, dry places such as roadsides, sandy fields and gravel pits, where it suns itself on ground. Flight short and fluttering. Two generations on wing May–June and August–September respectively. Females deposit about 50 eggs singly on plants such as meadow grass (*Poa*) and orchard grass (*Dactylis*). For larva: see no. 243.

135 *Lasiommata marea maera*
Large Wall Brown
Characteristics: Male: Wing length 22–28 mm. Topside brown with greyish tint. Forewing has big ocellus, often with double pupil, sometimes much smaller ocellus nearer edge. Post-discal section has faint reddish-yellow tint be-

tween veins. Scent-scale stripe fairly distinct. Topside of hind wing has 3 red-ringed ocelli, greyish-brown and brown markings and 5–6 brown-ringed ocelli on underside. Female (no. 135a) has distinct, reddish-yellow postdiscal band on topside of forewing. No. 135b shows male of southern European form, *adrasta*, very similar to female of *maera* form, but *adrasta* female has redder-brown forewings.

Distribution: Widespread in Europe, but less abundant and sometimes sporadic in north. Absent from British Isles, north Germany, Denmark and north-eastern area Scandinavia and Finland. Eastwards through Soviet Union to central Asia and Himalayas.

Habitat and Life History: Uncultivated, often stony terrain, surrounded by forests, often in mountains. In Scandinavia single generation June–July, further south in Europe two generations, first May–June, second August–September. Larva overwinters fully grown and lives on various grasses.

136 *Lasiommata petropolitana*
Northern Wall Brown
Characteristics: Male and female: Wing length 19–21 mm. Like small *maera* (no. 135), central cell on forewing has 2 obscure dark transverse lines, topside of hind wing has dark wavy line in discal section.

Distribution: Scandinavia and Finland (except far north-east), mountain areas in Alps, Pyrenees and Balkans. Also northern Soviet Union and northern Siberia.

Habitat and Life History: Open, stony localities in forest areas, in Alps up to 1,800 m. Single generation on wing May–July. Larva lives on grasses. Pupa overwinters.

137 *Lopinga achine*
Woodland Brown
Characteristics: Male and female: Wing length 25–28 mm. Easily recognised by greyish-brown topside with row of yellow-ringed, blind ocelli on both wings. Lighter underside with more distinct ocelli, often with white pupils.

Distribution: Scattered colonies from France and Belgium through central Germany, Poland and Soviet Union to Japan. Absent in southern Europe, British Isles, north-west Germany. Scandinavia, south-east Sweden and southern Finland.

Habitat and Life History: Open forest areas with rich grass vegetation. Single generation on wing June–July. Larva overwinters on various grasses.

LYCAENIDAE (BLUES)

The Lycaenidae are a very extensive family of mainly small butterflies, including the smallest of all. There are about 100 species in Europe, but world wide the family numbers thousands of species. The European blues divide into two sub-families. The first, Riodininae, represented by one species, *Hamearis lucina* (no. 138) is characterised by the male's reduced forelegs, similar to many Nymphalid species. The second sub-family, Lycaeninae, exhibits considerable difference between the sexes: the males are often blue or copper-coloured, whereas females are brown; but markings on the underside are fairly similar on both sexes, and help to identify the species. Some species can only be identified by their genitalia.

Lycaenidae larvae are characteristically short, broad and flattened, living on plants of the pea family. Many larvae live with ants, in a symbiosis which has developed to different degrees for individual species. For larvae: see nos. 244–249.

138 *Hamearis lucina*
Duke of Burgundy Fritillary
Characteristics: Male and female: Wing length 14–17 mm. Topside dark brown with transverse rows of reddish-yellow, angular spots, especially on forewings. Underside (no. 138a) of hind wing cinnamon-brown with white basal spots and band of white post-discal spots.
Distribution: Central Spain through central and southern Europe to central Soviet Union. Northern limit about 60°N, through southern England. Previously found in Scandinavia.
Habitat and Life History: Clearings in woods and uncultivated banks near woods. Single generation on

wing in northern part of range; May–June in southern Europe, two generations on wing May and August. Eggs deposited on back of primrose (*Primula*) leaves. Larva takes 6 weeks to develop fully, and then pupates. Pupa is fixed to leaf or stem from August through winter.

139 *Thecla betulae*
Brown Hairstreak
Characteristics: Male: Wing length 17–18 mm. Topside black-brown. On forewing black transverse line at end of central cell, outside which a faint orange section occasionally occurs. Hind wing has couple of small, orange spots near back margin. Underside (no. 139a)

ochre-yellow with greyish tint, on hind wing short, white discal line and longer post-discal line. Female (no. 139b) bigger with broad, orange-red band on forewing.

Distribution: Northern Spain and western Europe through central Europe, parts of southern and northern Europe, and east through Asia to Korea. Northern limit in Scandinavia and Finland about 62°N. Also southern England. Occasionally Iberian Peninsula, southern Italy or southern Balkans.

Habitat and Life History: On wing August–September, but only in sunny weather. The flight is rapid and vigorous. Eggs deposited singly near leaf-buds of sloe, plums and damsons. For larva: see no. 244.

140 *Quercusia quercus*
Purple Hairstreak

Characteristics: Male: Wing length 12–14 mm. Topside brown with purple-blue tint and black marginal border. Underside (no. 140a) greyish with white post-discal line, two yellow spots near back corner of hind wing, one with black pupil. Forewing sometimes has yellow spots near back corner in cells 1 and 2. Female (no. 140b) has bright, shiny violet basal spot on forewing.

Distribution: Southern, central and northern Europe as far north as 60°N. Much of British Isles and North Africa. East through Soviet Union and Asia Minor to Armenia.

Habitat and Life History: Favours extensive oak vegetation. Single generation July–August. Frequents crowns of trees, more abundant some years than others. Eggs deposited singly on oak twigs to overwinter. Larvae appear in spring, taking 6 weeks to develop fully. Pupation in moss and lichen on tree trunks and branches or between roots.

141 *Laeosopis roboris*
Spanish Purple Hairstreak

Characteristics: Male: Wing length 12–15 mm. Topside has very wide, brownish-black marginal border; inside which wings are dark purple-blue, less distinct on hind wing. Female larger and less purple-blue. Underside (no. 141a) yellowish-grey with orange-yellow margin. Inside margin black, triangular spots are surrounded by lighter spots.

Distribution: Spain, Portugal and south-east France.

Habitat and Life History: Hills and mountain slopes with sparse tree vegetation from sea level to 1,500 m. On wing late May to late August. Larva feeds on ash (*Fraxinus excelsior*), and is regarded as a forest pest in Spain.

142 *Nordmannia acaciae*
Sloe Hairstreak

Characteristics: Male and female:

Wing length 14–16 mm. Topside dark brown with no markings, short tail on hind wing. Underside (no. 142a) lighter brown with white post-discal line; orange marginal crescents, often with black edges, in cells 1a–3 on hind wing. *Distribution:* Northern Spain and southern Europe to southern Soviet Union and Asia Minor. Northern limit in Europe about 42°N.
Habitat and Life History: Uncultivated areas with sloe (*Prunus spinosus*) scrub, the larva's only food plant. On wing June–July and only common locally.

143 *Nordmannia esculi*
False Ilex Hairstreak
Characteristics: Male: Wing length 15–17 mm. Topside dark brown. Underside (no. 143a) lighter brown with irregular, white post-discal line and row of small, red spots in cells 1b–5, indistinctly ringed with black (cf. no. 144). Female bigger with occasional faint orange tinge in post-discal section on topside.
Distribution: Spain and Portugal, except northern coastal areas; also south-east France and North Africa.
Habitat and Life History: Same as no. 142. On wing June–July. Larva feeds on holm oak (*Quercus ilex*).

144 *Nordmannia ilicis*
Ilex Hairstreak
Characteristics: Male: Wing length

16–18 mm. Topside plain brown with small, orange spot near back corner of hind wing. Underside (no. 144a) has white post-discal line and red crescent spots edged with black. Female (no. 144b) usually has orange discal spot on forewing and larger, red crescent spots.
Distribution: Most of western, central and southern Europe, but not British Isles and very local on Iberian Peninsula. Northern limit through Denmark and southern Sweden.
Habitat and Life History: Warm, hilly terrain with scattered oak vegetation. On wing June–July, but difficult to spot. Larva overwinters on back of leaves of small oaks in sunny situations.

145 *Strymonidia spini*
Blue-spot Hairstreak
Characteristics: Male and female: Wing length 14–16 mm. Topside very similar to no. 144. Two orange marginal spots on hind wing. Underside has white post-discal line; blue spot and 2–3 orange marginal spots near back corner of hind wing. Females often bigger with clearer markings.
Distribution: Southern and central Europe to south-west Asia. Northern limit along southern coast of Baltic. Prefers uncultivated, hilly terrain with scattered scrub including *Prunus* and *Rhamnus* species, the larva's food plants. On wing June–July.

146 *Strymonidia w-album*
White-letter Hairstreak

Characteristics: Male: Wing length 15–16 mm. Topside brownish-black with small, pale, oval scent-scale spot near costal margin of forewing; occasional small orange spot in back corner of hind wing. Underside (no. 146a) has whitish post-discal line forming 'W' on hind wing, also with orange marginal spots. Female larger and paler.

Distribution: Southern British Isles and France through central and southern Europe east to Japan. Northern limit about 60°N, through south-east Norway and central Sweden. Not Finland or much of Iberian Peninsula.

Habitat and Life History: On wing June–August, with annual fluctuation in numbers. Frequents blackberry (*Rubus fruticosus*), nettle or thistle vegetation near elms (*Ulmus*), larva's food plant. Larva fully grown in 6 weeks.

147 *Strymonidia pruni*
Black Hairstreak

Characteristics: Male: Wing length 15–16 mm. Topside dark brown, forewing has small scent-scale spot, and couple of orange crescent spots on hind wing. Underside (no. 147a) of hind wing has orange band defined towards inside by distinct black spots. Light post-discal line on both wings. Female bigger often with orange tint on forewing.

Distribution: Local in central and western Europe, more abundant in eastern Europe. Eastwards to eastern Siberia and Korea. Northern limit through eastern Denmark, southern Sweden and southern Finland. Westwards to line from Kiel (Germany) to Bay of Biscay. Isolated population in eastern British Isles. Mostly absent from southern Europe.

Habitat and Life History: Frequents open woods and scrub with sloe, (*Prunus spinosus*) vegetation on which larva lives. Single generation on wing June–July. Eggs deposited on sloe branches, often fairly low down. Larva emerges following April, and eats sloe buds. After a couple of months it pupates on leaf or branch, resembling bird dropping.

148 *Callophrys rubi*
Green Hairstreak

Characteristics: Male and female: Wing length 13–15 mm. Topside light or dark greyish-brown. Margin of hind wing wavy with alternating light and dark fringe sections. Underside (no. 148a) bright green, forewing greyish-brown near back, hind wing has few small, white spots.

Distribution: Throughout Europe (common all over British Isles), Soviet Union and northern Asia.

Habitat and Life History: Boggy areas and scrub, edges of woodland and ditches with rich vegetation. Usually on wing late

May–June. Short, swift flight. Often rests on green leaves, with folded wings, thus difficult to see. Eggs deposited singly on buds, notably blackberry (*Rubus fruticosus*), broom (*Cytisus*) and whortleberry (*Vaccinium*) species. For larva: see no. 245.

149 *Tomares ballus*
Provence Hairstreak
Characteristics: Male: Wing length 14–15 mm. Topside light greyish-brown with small orange spots on hind wing in cells 1b and 2. Underside (no. 149a) of forewing edged with light greyish-brown; orange discal section with black spots. Female (no. 149b) has extensive orange areas on fore- and hind wings.
Distribution: Iberian Peninsula (except north) and locally in southern France. Also North Africa.
Habitat and Life History: Uncultivated, stony places from sea level to about 1,500 m. Single generation on wing in February on coast, in April at higher altitudes. Larva lives on hairy birdsfoot-trefoil (*Lotus hispidus*).

150 *Lycaena helle*
Violet Copper
Characteristics: Male: Wing length 12–14 mm. Topside covered with violet dust, rather obscuring orange, greyish-brown ground. Orange-red crescent spots on hind wing defined by black spots either side. Underside (no. 150a) orange-yellowish-grey with small, black spots and rows of spots and prominent orange-red marginal bands. Female (no. 150b) lacks violet tint of male.
Distribution: Central Sweden, Norway north of Oslo, and throughout Finland. Scattered colonies from France and Belgium through Bavaria, eastern Germany, Poland, Czechoslovakia, and eastwards through Soviet Union to Siberia. Very local and declining with progressive loss of habitat.
Habitat and Life History: Wet meadows, bogs, swamps and forest edges with ditches. Single Scandinavian generation on wing May–June; in central Europe small second generation sometimes apparent in autumn. Eggs deposited singly on knotgrass (*Polygonum*) and other food plants where pupa overwinters.

151 *Lycaena phlaeas*
Small Copper
Characteristics: Male and female: Wing length 12–15 mm. Topside of forewing gleams golden-red with 2 black spots in central cell, irregular post-discal row of spots, and fairly wide brownish-black marginal band. Topside of hind wing brownish-black with red marginal border from back corner to cell 5. Underside (no. 151a) of forewing light orange-yellow with black, yellow-ringed spots and greyish-brown marginal band.

Underside of hind wing greyish-brown with obscure darker spots and reddish marginal crescents.

Distribution: Throughout Europe and temperate areas of Asia to Japan.

Habitat and Life History: Mainly grass fields with flowers and ditches. Two or three generations on wing May–June, July–August and September–October. In southern Europe on wing as early as February–March. For larva: see no. 246.

152 *Lycaena dispar*
Large Copper

Characteristics: Male: Wing length 17–20 mm. Topside gleams golden-red with narrow black marginal edge and narrow spot near top of central cell of forewing. Underside (no. 152a) of forewing light orange-yellow with black, white-ringed spots, and narrow, greyish marginal band. Underside of hind wing greyish-blue with red marginal band and black, white-tinged spots. Female (no. 152b) has darker topside.

Distribution: France, Po valley of Italy, northern Holland, eastern Germany, Poland, Baltic States, parts of Balkans, and throughout Soviet Union and Siberia. Local and rare because of declining habitat. In British Isles only just surviving in Wood Walton Fen, Huntingdonshire.

Habitat and Life History: Bogs and swamps; drainage threatens survival and population unstable anyway. Single generation on wing June–July. Larva feeds on water dock (*Rumex hydrolapathum*), and other dock species, where it overwinters. Can tolerate submergence. Feeds for 2 weeks after hibernation, then pupates. Butterfly emerges 2 weeks later.

153 *Heodes tityrus*
Sooty Copper

Characteristics: Male: Wing length 14–16 mm. Topside black-brown with small, black spots and indistinct orange spots along margin. Underside of forewing light orange-yellow, underside of hind wing yellower-grey, both with small, black spots, also orange marginal band on hind wing. Female (no. 153a) more orange-brown on topside; orange band with round, black spots separated from margin on hind wing.

Distribution: Southern and central Europe as far north as eastern Denmark. Parts of Iberian Peninsula; east through Soviet Union to central Asia. Very local.

Habitat and Life History: Dry, sandy soil near forests. Two generations on wing visiting flowers April–May and July–September. Larva overwinters on species of dock (*Rumex*).

154 *Heodes virgaureae*
Scarce Copper

Characteristics: Male: Wing length 16–17 mm. Topside gleams

golden-red, margin and underside of hind wing yellowish-grey. Both wings have black spots, hind wing has white post-discal spots. Female (no. 154b) distinctly dark on topside.
Distribution: Mainly central Europe. Eastwards through Soviet Union and central Asia to Mongolia.
Habitat and Life History: Meadows and fields with flowers, from lowlands to 1,500 m. Single generation on wing July–August. Flight fast and steady. Eggs deposited singly on stems of dock (*Rumex*) species; overwinter to April. For larva: see no. 247.

155 *Heodes alciphron alciphron*
Purple-shot Copper
Characteristics: Male: Wing length 16–18 mm. Orange-red ground of topside covered with heavy violet tinge. More or less distinct rows of post-discal spots on both wings. Underside yellow-grey to blue-grey with numerous black, white-ringed spots and orange marginal band on hind wing. Female (no. 155a) bigger, dark brown with obscure, darker spots and orange spots in cells 1b–6 of hind wing.
Distribution: South of Baltic from eastern France through Germany, Czechoslovakia and Poland to Soviet Union. Replaced in south by no. 156.
Habitat and Life History: Dry, warm localities with flowers. Single gene-

ration on wing June–July. Larva overwinters on dock (*Rumex*) species and pupates underground.

156 *Heodes alciphron gordius*
Swiss Purple-shot Copper
Characteristics: Like no. 155, but fainter violet tinge and bigger dark spots on topside. Female (no. 156a) orange-red with strong spot markings and faint dark dust.
Distribution, Habitat and Life History: Replaces previous species in southern Europe, mainly in mountain areas from 1,200 to 1,800 m. On wing June–August.

157 *Thersamonia thersamon*
Lesser Fiery Copper
Characteristics: Male: Wing length 14–16 mm. Topside light golden-red; forewing without distinct spots but has narrow, black border; hind wing slightly shaded with several black spots in marginal band which fuse with narrow border. Underside of forewing light orange with typical spot pattern. Underside of hind wing light blue-grey with orange marginal band defined by rows of black spots. Female has distinct spots on topside.
Distribution: South-east Europe north to Bohemia, and parts of mainland Italy. Eastwards through western Asia to Iraq and Iran.

Habitat and Life History: Open, uncultivated places up to 1,200 m; two generations on wing April–May and July–August. Larva lives on dock (*Rumex*) and broom (*Cytisus*).

158 *Palaeochrysophanus hippothoe hippothoe*
Purple-edged Copper

Characteristics: Male: Wing length 16–17 mm. Topside dark flamered with deep violet, gleaming edges, especially along costal margin, and on dark hind wing. Underside grey to greyish-orange with typical spot markings. Female (no. 158a) has extensive dark dust on topside, while post-discal spots on forewing form regular curve. Hind wing has orange marginal border enclosing black spots.

Distribution: Throughout Scandinavia and Finland (replaced by subspecies *stiperi* in most northerly part), central European mountain areas, northern Spain and northern Italy. Eastwards through Soviet Union and Siberia to Pacific. Very local in restricted areas. Population declining. See also no. 159.

Habitat and Life History: Damp forest meadows and bogs. Single generation on wing about June–July. Eggs deposited singly on underside of dock (*Rumex*) leaves and knotgrass (*Polygonum*). Young larva overwinters; fully grown by May.

159 *Palaeochrysophanus hippothoe eurydame*

Characteristics: Male: Wing length 16–17 mm. Distinguished from no. 158 by warm golden topside, with narrow dark margin but no violet tinge. Female darker with faint orange markings.

Distribution: Replaces no. 158 in western Alps, south of Rhône valley. Also mountain areas in Italy.

Habitat and Life History: Mountain meadows from 1,500 to 2,000 m. On wing June–August.

160 *Lampides boeticus*
Long-tailed Blue

Characteristics: Male: Wing length 15–18 mm. Topside violet-blue somewhat clouded by dark scent scales. Hind wing has 2 black spots and thin tail. Underside (no. 160a) pale brown with paler, transverse, wavy lines and spots. Hind wing has broader light post-discal stripe and two black and turquoise ocelli. Female (no. 160b) brown with bluish basal area.

Distribution: South Europe and North Africa with late summer migration to central Europe and as far north as south coast of British Isles, Holland and southern Germany.

Habitat and Life History: Uncultivated places with rich herb vegetation, also flowering lucerne fields. In southern Europe to 2,000 m and above. Two generations on wing from spring to late autumn. Larva lives in pods of various species of pea family.

161 *Syntarucus pirithous*
Lang's Short-tailed Blue
Characteristics: Male: Wing length 12–13 mm. Topside blue, often with brownish tinge where scales rubbed off. Couple of obscure black spots near corner of hind wing. Underside (no. 161a) brownish with irregular pattern of paler, transverse, wavy stripes and bands. Hind wing has two turquoise ocelli with black pupils. Female (no. 161b) more grey-brown, bluish near base, but otherwise similar to male.
Distribution: Southern Europe, including southern France and south slopes of Alps. Parts of Mediterranean coast.
Habitat and Life History: Similar to no. 160 which it often accompanies. Frequents mountain areas to 2,000 m. Several generations on wing late March to late autumn. Tends to migrate. Larva feeds on various species of pea family, notably broom (*Cytisus*), flowers of which the butterfly visits.

162 *Everes argiades*
Short-tailed Blue
Characteristics: Male: Wing length 10–15 mm. Topside violet-blue with narrow black margin; often 2 dark spots near corner of hind wing, with its thin tail. Underside (no. 162a) light grey with small black spots; space between marginal spots in cells 1c and 2 on hind wing orange. Female has bluish-black topside with blue dust in basal section and orange spot near corner of hind wing.
Distribution: Northern Spain across southern and central Europe through Asia to Japan. Northern limit in Europe about 52°N. Some migration in northern Europe; migrants on southern downs in British Isles from May to September.
Habitat and Life History: Open, flowery places, often fairly damp, up to 1,000 m. Two or three generations on wing from April. Larva overwinters on various plants of pea family.

163 *Cupido osiris*
Osiris Blue
Characteristics: Male: Wing length 12–15 mm. Topside fairly dark violet-blue with very narrow, black marginal line. Underside light grey, often blue at base, with row of black spots (cf. no. 164a). Female dark brown with blue tinge on topside of forewing.
Distribution: Central and northern Spain through southern France to Switzerland and northern Italy through Balkans and Asia Minor to central Asia.
Habitat and Life History: Mountain slopes with rich flower vegetation from 750 to 1,800 m. One or two generations on wing from late

May. Larva feeds on various plants of pea family.

164 *Cupido minimus*
   Small Blue

Characteristics: Male: Wing length 10-12 mm. Topside dark brown with slight bluish tinge. Underside (no. 164a) grey, often with bluish-green tinge near base, and small, white-ringed black spots, forming straight row on forewing and wavy line on hind wing. Female lacks bluish tinge on topside.

Distribution: Widespread in Europe and Asia to the Pacific. Absent from northern Scandinavia, and parts of north Germany, Holland and southern Spain. Common but local in southern British Isles.

Habitat and Life History: Dry, uncultivated places, such as gravel pits. Single generation on wing May-July in northern Europe, two generations further south. Favours various small plants of pea family, such as kidney vetch (*Anthyllis*). For larva: see no. 248.

165 *Celastrina argiolus*
   Holly Blue

Characteristics: Male: Wing length 13-17 mm. Topside pale blue with narrow dark chequered margin. Underside (no. 165a) whitish-grey with bluish basal section and small black oblique spots on forewing. Males of second brood darker blue with broader dark margins. Female (no. 165b) has paler blue topside and broad

dark marginal band on forewing.
Distribution: Throughout Europe, except north-western Scandinavia and Finland. Eastwards to central Asia and Japan. Also North America.

Habitat and Life History: Woodland clearings, some forest bogs. Two generations in April-May and July-August, usually most abundant mid-May. On wing fairly high, seeking tree sap, manure and carrion. Larva lives on flowers of various bushes; in Europe spring brood feeds on holly (*Ilex aquifolium*) or dogwood (*Thelycrania sanguinea*). Autumn brood always on ivy (*Hedera helix*). Pupa overwinters.

166 *Glaucopsyche alexis*
   Green-underside Blue

Characteristics: Male: Wing length 13-18 mm. Topside blue with relatively broad, black margin. Underside (no. 166a) greyish without marginal spots, bluish-green near base, with curved row of black spots on forewing, diminishing in size from cell 2 towards costa. Female has brown topside and bluish tint at base.

Distribution: Northern Spain and France east through southern and central Europe to Soviet Union and eastern Siberia. Also south-east Norway, eastern and central Sweden and southern and central Finland.

Habitat and Life History: Open sunny places surrounded by trees and scrub, between hills, on sunken roads or in forest clearings. Single generation on wing June–July in north of range, in southern Europe two generations on wing earlier. Tiny larva overwinters on plants of pea family, usually the larger varieties.

167 *Maculinea alcon alcon and alcon rebeli*
Alcon Blue

Characteristics: Male: Wing length 17–19 mm. Topside pale blue to pale grey-blue with narrow dark margin. Underside (no. 167a) grey-blue to grey-brown with dark light-ringed spots; basal area tinged bluish-green in some populations. Topside of female (no. 167b) grey-brown, basal area more or less blue, sometimes with row of dark spots parallel to margin.

Distribution: Northern Spain and France eastwards through central and eastern Europe to central Asia. Northern limit through Denmark and southern Sweden. Local in Italy and Balkans. Two subspecies form intermediate populations.

Habitat and Life History: Damp moors and bogs, also dry, sandy places. Single generation usually on wing July–August. Larva lives for 2 months inside flower of gentian (*Gentiana*) species. In September moves into ants' nest to overwinter, feeding on ants' larvae and pupae, while ants suck nectar secreted by *alcon* larvae and pupae. Pupates in ants' nest.

168 *Maculinea arion*
Large Blue

Characteristics: Male: Wing length 16–12 mm. Topside deep blue with broader marginal border than no. 167, usually with distinct dark post-discal spots on forewing, less distinct spots on hind wing. Underside (no. 168a) greyish, often with brown tinge, bluish-green base, and large, distinct black spots. Female similar to male, but bigger spots on topside of forewing. Mountain populations sometimes very dark on topside.

Distribution: France through central and southern Europe, Soviet Union and Siberia to China. Northern limit through central Sweden and southern Finland about 60°N. Local in southern British Isles, in 3 or 4 small colonies in Somerset and Gloucestershire; Holland and north-west Germany. Restricted to mountain areas in central and northern Spain.

Habitat and Life History: Dry, sandy hills with heather and grass vegetation, also near coasts. Single generation on wing June–August. Eggs deposited singly on flowers of thyme (*Thymus*). Tiny larva very similar to flowers. Although casts skin three times, larva only 3 mm long. But leaves plant and eventually 'milked' by ant and taken to ant-hill, where larva feeds on ant larvae and pupae until following spring. It pupates inside ants' nest in May.

169 *Maculinea teleius*
Scarce Large Blue
Characteristics: Male: Wing length 17–18 mm. Topside similar to no. 168, but with smaller, often obscure post-discal spots. Underside (no. 169a) light brown, with no bluish-green in basal area; black spots fairly small and obscure except post-discal spots. Female darker blue on topside with broader brown-black section along costal and outer margin. Underside slightly darker.
Distribution: North-east France and south Holland in narrow band eastwards through Germany (not north of Berlin area) and Switzerland. Across central eastern Europe to Asia and Japan. Southward limit on southern alpine slopes.
Habitat and Life History: Very local, but often numerous in suitable habitat, such as swamps and wet meadows; up to about 2,000 m. Single generation on wing late June–August. Larva lives at first on great burnet (*Sanguisorba officinalis*), later with ants.

170 *Maculinea nausithous*
Dusky Large Blue
Characteristics: Male: Wing length 17–18 mm. Topside somewhat darker than *teleius* (no. 169), with broader, black marginal border and often fewer spots. Underside also darker, almost cinnamon-brown, without marginal spots. Female completely dark brown, occasionally tinged with blue in basal area, no spots on topside.
Distribution: Almost identical to no. 169, from north-eastern France through Germany to Poland and Czechoslovakia. Isolated occurrence in Spain.
Habitat and Life History: Swampy lowland areas, often near lakes. Single generation on wing June–August. For larva: see no. 169.

171 *Iolana iolas*
Iolas Blue
Characteristics: Male: Wing length 18–21 mm. Topside lustrous violet-blue with no spots, but narrow dark marginal border. Underside light grey, often with slightly blue-green basal area, forewing striped in discal section. Black, white-ringed post-discal spots noticeably closer to margin on forewing than hind wing. Marginal spots obscure. Female (no. 171a) has broad greyish-brown area along margins on both wings.
Distribution: Mountain areas in Spain, south-east France, Rhône valley in Switzerland, northern and central Italy, also Balkans north to lower Austria and east through Asia Minor to Iran. Also North Africa.
Habitat and Life History: Uncul-

tivated, stony areas, preferably with scattered trees and scrub, up to 1,800 m. Usually only one generation, on wing May–June, occasional small second brood on wing August–September. Larva lives in pods of bladder senna (*Colutea arborescens*).

172 *Philotes baton*
Baton Blue
Characteristics: Male: Wing length 10–12 mm. Topside light blue with grey tinge at tip of forewing, black discal spot on both wings, and black marginal spots on hind wing. Underside (no. 172a) grey or brownish-grey with prominent black spots; row of orange marginal crescents on hind wing, but missing on populations in central and southern Spain (subspecies *panoptus*). Female brownish-black, with variable blue dust in basal area.
Distribution: Europe up to 48°N; not British Isles, Netherlands, north-west Germany, Scandinavia or Finland. Rare, closely-related species, *Philotus baton schiffermuelleri*, only distinguishable by genital characteristics, found in southern Finland; also replaces *baton* parts of eastern Europe as far west as central Germany.
Habitat and Life History: Uncultivated, dry terrain with herb vegetation, up to 2,000 m. One or two generations depending on altitude. On wing April–June and July–September. Larva feeds

on thyme (*Thymus*) at first, later lives with ants.

173 *Scoliantides orion*
Chequered Blue
Characteristics: Male: Wing length 13–16 mm. Topside very dark, forewing has variable amount of blue in basal area; marginal crescents of hind wing have blue inner edges; fringes are clearly chequered black and white. Underside (no. 173a) whitish-grey with very prominent jet black spots; hind wing has band of orange marginal crescents. Female usually lacks markings on topside.
Distribution: Partly southern Europe as far north as 50°N; mountain areas in Spain, south-east France, Switzerland, northern Italy and Balkans, partly in narrow band from southern Norway across Sweden to southern Finland. East through central Asia to Japan.
Habitat and Life History: Dry, stony, warm places, especially on calcareous soil up to 900 m. Single generation in north on wing July in lowlands and warmer places; two generations in south on wing May–June and August. Larva feeds on stonecrop (*Sedum*). Pupa overwinters in top soil under stones or leaves.

174 *Plebeius argus*
Silver-studded Blue
Characteristics: Male: Wing length

12–15 mm. Topside dark-blue with relatively broad, black marginal border (cf. no. 175). Underside pale smoky grey, blue at base, with black, white-ringed spots and orange marginal crescents. Distinguished from no. 175 by strong spur on topside of fore-tibia. Female (no. 174a) bronze-brown with orange, marginal crescents; often blue dust at base of wing. Underside has heavier markings than no. 175.

Distribution: Most of Europe. In British Isles only in south; absent from northern and north-western Scandinavia and Finland. Northern limit about 68°N. Variations in Alps, Spanish mountains and Sardinia and Corsica. Eastwards through temperate areas of Asia to Japan.

Habitat and Life History: Dry, poor soil, on heaths, hills and slopes. Single generation on wing July–August in northern Europe, in central and southern Europe two generations on wing from May. Often swarms, particularly at night and flies fairly low. Eggs deposited in August overwinter to following April. Larva eats flowers of various plants, especially pea family. Development takes three months; pupal stage lasts 2–3 weeks.

175 *Lycaeides idas*
   Idas Blue
Characteristics: Male: Wing length 14–16 mm. Similar to no. 174,

but dark marginal border on topside narrower and better defined, and fore-tibia only has small spur. Underside has less distinct markings, its ground colour more yellow-brown and spots obscure. Female (no. 175a) brown, base variously blue often with prominent orange marginal crescents. Underside of female darker with more contrasts than male. Species varies considerably; several subspecies have been described.

Distribution: Throughout Europe, except British Isles and parts of Spain and Portugal.

Habitat and Life History: Similar to no. 175 with which it often flies. In northern and central Europe single generation on wing June to August, in southern Europe two generations. Larva's host plants various species of pea family; transported by ants, larva overwinters in their nest.

Lycaeides argyrognomon
Reverdin's Blue
Only distinguished with certainty, from close relative *idas* (no. 175) by genital characteristics. But note black marginal V-spots inside gently curved orange marginal crescents on underside of hind wing, unlike acute-angled crescents on *idas*. Found south Norway and south-east Sweden, also central and south-east Europe and Italy.

176 *Vacciniina optilete*
Cranberry Blue
Characteristics: Male: Wing length 13–15 mm. Topside plain deep violet-blue with narrow black marginal line. Underside (no. 176a) greyish with prominent black spots and red spot with blue scales in cell 2 of hind wing, occasionally in adjacent cells also. Female dark brown with variable violet tinge at base; occasional orange spot in cell 2 on topside of hind wing.
Distribution: Scandinavia and Finland, but also Holland, Germany, Poland and Czechoslovakia. Also Alps, and isolated mountain colonies in Balkans. Eastwards through northern Soviet Union and Siberia to Japan.
Habitat and Life History: Bogs and quagmires, a diminishing habitat. Also mountain slopes. Single generation on wing July. Larva lives on cranberry (*Vaccinium oxycoccus*), and other *Vaccinium* species, also bell-heather (*Erica*). Tiny larva overwinters.

177 *Eumedonia eumedon*
Geranium Argus
Characteristics: Male: Wing length 14–16 mm. Topside plain dark brown. Ground colour of underside (no. 177a) grey or grey-brown, with post-discal spots on forewing forming straight line. White line along vein no. 5, blue dust at base, and small, indistinct orange marginal crescents on hind wing. Female bigger with occasional obscure orange marginal crescents near corner of hind wing.
Distribution: Mountain areas in northern Spain and France. From Alps north to Baltic; also Sweden and Norway, except western coastal areas. Finland east through Soviet Union and Siberia to Pacific.
Habitat and Life History: Dry meadows, uncultivated grassy fields, dry slopes and mountain sides. Single generation on wing June–July. Larva lives on cranesbill (*Geranium*) species.

178 *Aricia agestis*
Brown Argus
Characteristics: Male and female: Wing length 12–14 mm. Topside dark brown with complete row of orange marginal spots on both wings; spots biggest on female. Underside (no. 178a) greyish or light brownish-grey with prominent black, white-ringed spots. Black post-discal spot in cell 6 of hind wing displaced towards base. Row of orange-red sub-marginal spots on both wings.
Distribution: Southern and central Europe with northern limit through English Midlands, Denmark and southern Sweden. Occasionally in Scotland. Not Finland or Iberian Peninsula.
Habitat and Life History: Open terrain with natural grass and herb vegetation, mountain areas

up to about 900 m. Two generations on wing May–June and
July–August in central Europe.
Three generations in southern
Europe. Visits flowers in warm,
sunny weather. Brisk flight. Eggs
deposited on cranesbill (*Geranium*), storksbill (*Erodium*), and
rock rose (*Helianthemum*). Larva
overwinters. Larva's nectar gland
visited by ants, themselves probably vital to larva. Pupa lies free
on ground under host plants;
pupal stage lasts 2 weeks.

179 *Aricia agestis artaxerxes*
   Scotch Argus
Characteristics: Male and female:
Wing length 11–12 mm. Very
similar to no. 178, besides white
discal spot on forewing, smaller
orange marginal spots on topside
sometimes missing altogether from
forewing, especially on male. Black
pupils in ocelli on underside much
reduced, making spots seem almost
white. Distinct orange submarginal spots.
Distribution: British Isles, especially
Scotland.
Habitat and Life History: See no. 180.

180 *Aricia artaxerxes inhonora*

Characteristics: Male: Wing length
14–16 mm, larger than no. 179.
Topside of forewing dark brown,
usually without marginal crescents. Topside of hind wing has
small, obscure, orange crescents in
cells 1c, 2, 3 and 4. Underside

greyish or brownish with typical
spot pattern, but some variation.
Female often larger with more
prominent orange spots on topside;
underside darker than male.
Distribution: Eastern Europe, also
most of Scandinavia and Finland,
with western limit in Denmark
and Germany (Harz mountains).
Subspecies *allous* (usually without
crescents in cell 4) found in
mountain areas of central Europe.
Habitat and Life History: Dry and
sandy, preferably calcareous, soil.
Single generation on wing July–
August. Larva lives on cranesbill
(*Geranium*) species.

181 *Aricia cramera*
   Southern Brown Argus
Characteristics: Male and female:
Wing length 11–13 mm. Very
similar to *agestis* (no. 178), but
much bigger orange-red marginal
crescents on topside, especially in
female.
Distribution: Iberian Peninsula and
North Africa.
Habitat and Life History: Mountain
slopes and other uncultivated
terrain. Several generations on
wing from April throughout summer. Host plant of larva notably
rock rose (*Helianthemum*) and
species of clover (*Trifolium*).

182 *Aricia nicias*
   Silvery Argus
Characteristics: Male: Wing length
11–12 mm. Topside ice-blue with
broad, brown marginal border.

Underside (no. 182a) light grey with small, indistinct black and white ocelli; hind wing has white mark along vein 4, and obscure marginal spots. Topside of female brown, but underside similar to male.

Distribution: Two separate areas. Partly southern Finland and eastern Sweden north of Stockholm; partly eastern Pyrenees and southwestern Alps in France and southern Switzerland.

Habitat and Life History: Open, sunny places surrounded by hardwood forest, in lowland Sweden and Finland, in southern European mountain areas between 900 and 1,500 m. Single generation on wing in July, but generally rare. Larva feeds mainly on meadow cranesbill (*Geranium pratense*). Eggs overwinter.

183 *Albulina orbitulus*
Alpine Argus

Characteristics: Male: Wing length 12–14 mm. Topside shiny blue with very narrow black border. Underside (no. 183a) greyish; wings have white spots, without usual black pupils. Marginal spots very obscure. Female predominantly brown on topside, often with slight blue tinge at base; underside paler brown with markings similar to male.

Distribution: Two separate areas. Partly Sweden and Norway, partly high Alps. Also mountain areas in Asia.

Habitat and Life History: Mountain slopes rich with flowers between 500 and 1,400 m in Norway and Sweden, from 1,600 m in the Alps. Single generation on wing July–August. Larva lives on species of milk vetch (*Astragalus*).

184 *Cyaniris semiargus*
Mazarine Blue

Characteristics: Male: Wing length 14–17 mm. Topside dark violet blue with moderately broad, fairly blurred darker marginal border. Underside (no. 184a) greyish-brown, greenish-blue at base of wings, with small spots; marginal spots completely missing, though occasional traces of marginal markings near corner of hind wing. Topside of female brown, but underside similar to male.

Distribution: Throughout Europe, except northern Scandinavia and Finland (north of 68°N) and parts of Iberian Peninsula. Migrant on south coast of British Isles. Eastwards through Soviet Union and central Asia to Mongolia.

Habitat and Life History: Meadows, fields and uncultivated places, often near coast. Single generation on wing mainly in July. Larva lives inside flowers on members of pea family, such as clover (*Trifolium*) and kidney vetch (*Anthyllis*). Hibernates as early as August. Fully grown following May. Pupation on host plant.

185 *Agrodiaetus damon*
Damon Blue

Characteristics: Male: Wing length 15–17 mm. Topside shiny pale blue, greyish-brown broad marginal border. Underside (no. 185a) light greyish-brown, curved row of 5–6 post-discal ocelli each surrounding discal spot on forewing. On hind wing characteristic light line along vein 4, also tiny, indistinct ocelli. Topside of female brown, with occasional tinge of blue at base; underside similar to male.
Distribution: Central Spain, and north-west from Pyrenees to Bavaria, the northern limit in Europe. Also central Italian mountains, Balkans, through Soviet Union and Armenia to Altai mountains.
Habitat and Life History: Local and sporadic; mainly mountain meadows and grassy slopes on calcareous soil. In Alps up to 2,000 m and over. Single generation on wing July–August. Larva overwinters on plants of pea family, especially sainfoin (*Onbry-chis*). Visited by ants.

Agrodiaetus dolus
Furry Blue

Larger than no. 185; wing length 17–19 mm. Topside of forewing has large, light scent-scale spot at base, and shorter, less distinct white line on underside of hind wing. Same habitats, but restricted to southern France and central Italian mountains.

186 *Agrodiaetus ripartii*
Ripart's Blue

Characteristics: Male: Wing length 14–17 mm. Plain brown on topside. Underside light yellowish-brown with 4 small discal spots on forewing; no distinct marginal spots. Hind wing has narrow white line along vein 4, and tiny ocelli. Female often has orange marginal crescents on topside near corner of hind wing, with more definite markings on underside than male.
Distribution: North-east Spain, south-east France and neighbouring parts of Italy. Also Balkans and Asia Minor.
Habitat and Life History: Warm mountain slopes with scrub, often at fairly low altitudes. On wing July–August. Larva lives on rock sainfoin (*Onobrychis saxatilis*).

187 *Plebicula escheri escheri*
Escher's Blue

Characteristics: Male: Wing length 17–19 mm. Topside sky blue with narrow black marginal line and whitish fringes, white costal and veins. Underside light grey with typical spot pattern and distinct black marginal line, often tinged with bluish-green dust in basal section. Female (no. 187a) brown with complete row of orange marginal spots on both wings; hind wing occasionally tinged blue near base. Underside similar to male.
Distribution: Mountain areas in Portugal, Spain, south-east

France, northern and central Italy, with north limit in southern Swiss alpine valleys. Also Balkans. *Habitat and Life History:* Scattered colonies preferably in warm, stony mountain slopes up to 2,000 m. Single generation on wing from June to August. Larva lives on species of milk vetch (*Astragalus*) and overwinters.

188 *Plebicula dorylas*
Turquoise Blue
Characteristics: Male: Wing length 15–17 mm. Topside difficult to distinguish from no. 187. Underside (no. 188a) greyish or yellowish, normally with smaller spots than *escheri*; black marginal line very indistinct, and margin edged with broad white band. Wedge-shaped spot near vein 4 on hind wing. Female brown, usually with orange marginal crescents on hind wing, often with blue dust in basal section. Underside similar to male.
Distribution: South-eastern Europe and Sweden with western limit from northern Spain through southern and eastern France to Baltic coast in Poland. Also through Balkans to Asia Minor.
Habitat and Life History: Local and uncommon. Favours calcareous soil in warm places rich with flowers, or sandy places, often with scattered scrub. Two generations on wing May–June and August–September; single generation in north and at high alti-

tudes, on wing in mid-summer. Larva overwinters in flower heads of pea species, especially kidney vetch (*Anthyllis*).

189 *Plebicula amanda*
Amanda's Blue
Characteristics: Male: Wing length 16–19 mm. Topside shiny ice-blue with broad, blurred, brownish-grey marginal border; similarly brownish-grey along veins towards base. Underside (no. 189a) greyish or brownish, with bluish-green at base; small post-discal spots on both wings; hind wing has orange marginal crescents in cells 1c, 2 and 3, inside small ante-marginal spots in cells 1–7. Topside of female brown, with orange crescents and black marginal spots in cells 1c–3 on hind wing. Often blue dust in basal section. Underside has darker ground than male.
Distribution: Throughout Europe, except west. Mountain areas in Iberian Peninsula. Scandinavia and Finland north to about 65°N. Western Asia to Iran. On decline.
Habitat and Life History: Hilly areas with scrub and bogs. Single generation on wing June–August. Tiny larva overwinters on tufted vetch (*Vicia cracca*). After hibernation eats till pupation in mid-May.

190 *Meleageria daphnis*
Meleager's Blue
Characteristics: Male: Wing length

18–19 mm. Topside very pale blue with sheen and fairly broad margin; hind wing characteristically scalloped between veins 2 and 3. Underside pale grey with grey marginal spots and black discoidal spots. No orange marginal crescents. Darker blue female (no. 190a) has even more deeply scalloped hind wing, broader margin and black ante-marginal spots on hind wing. Darker ground on underside than male.

Distribution: South-east Europe west to south-east France; also Rhône valley, Switzerland and much of mainland Italy. Eastwards through Asia Minor to Iran.

Habitat and Life History: Local on warm slopes to about 1,500 m. Single generation each year, on wing June–July. Larva feeds on milk vetch (*Astragalus*) and species of sainfoin (*Onobrychis*).

191 *Lysandra coridon*
Chalk-hill Blue
Characteristics: Male: Wing length 15–18 mm. Topside light silvery-blue. Forewing has fairly broad, dark marginal border and ante-marginal spots. Underside of forewing light grey with typical spot pattern. Underside of hind wing browner-grey, with blue-green dust, small black spots, and white, wedge-shaped mark extending to pale, obscure orange marginal crescents. Female (no. 191a) has brown topside, with occasional

blue dust; on hind wing 3–4 faint orange marginal crescents inside black ante-marginal spots. Underside similar to male, but darker with more definite markings.

Distribution: Across Europe from southern British Isles, France and Pyrenees north to southern coast of Baltic; eastwards to Soviet Union.

Habitat and Life History: Fairly abundant in dry meadows and grass-covered slopes on calcareous soil; up to 2,000 m in Alps. Single generation on wing July–August. Larva lives and overwinters on plants of pea family, particularly horseshoe vetch (*Hippocrepis comosa*). Larva often visited by ants.

192 *Lysandra albicans*
Spanish Chalk-hill Blue
Characteristics: Male: Wing length 18–21 mm. Topside very pale whitish-grey, sometimes tinged blue near base. Both wings have double marginal lines enclosing dark marginal spots. Underside very pale with small, indistinct spots. Female brown with orange marginal crescents inside dark, marginal spots. Underside brown with more prominent spots than male.

Distribution: Eastern and southern Spain and North Africa.

Habitat and Life History: Warm, rocky mountain slopes up to 1,500 m and over. On wing June–July. Host plants of larva unknown.

193 *Lysandra bellargus*
Adonis Blue

Characteristics: Male: Wing length 16–19 mm. Topside shiny blue, with very narrow dark margin, and chequered fringes. Underside (no. 193a) greyish-brown; extra spot in central cell of forewing; small orange marginal crescents on hind wing. Topside of female brown, often with blue dust and orange marginal crescents. Underside has darker ground.

Distribution: Widespread in Europe, with northern limit in southern British Isles, north-west Germany and along southern coast of Baltic. Rare in southern Spain and southern Italy. East through southern Soviet Union to Iraq and Iran.

Habitat and Life History: Grassy lowlands on calcareous soil, and up to about 2,000 m. Two generations on wing May–June and August–September. For larva: see no. 249.

194 *Polyommatus icarus*
Common Blue

Characteristics: Male: Wing length 14–18 mm. Topside sky blue with violet tinge. Underside (no. 194a) grey with greenish-blue dust in basal section. Besides typical, distinct spots, further one in central cell of forewing, another at base of cell 1b. Female (no. 194b) brown with violet-blue dust, especially in basal section; normally has orange marginal crescents and black ante-marginal spots on hind wing. Underside darker with more definite markings than male.

Distribution: Throughout Europe from Mediterranean to Arctic Ocean. Eastwards through temperate areas of Soviet Union and northern Asia. Also North Africa.

Habitat and Life History: Grassy places with flowers, including lawns. Two generations on wing May to September. Eggs deposited on plants of pea family, notably birdsfoot trefoil (*Lotus corniculatus*), and clover (*Trifolium*). Larva lives on underside of leaves. First brood hibernates September till March–April. Larva of second brood develops in 6 weeks. Pupa lies at foot of host plant, spun into light cocoon; pupal stage lasts about 2 weeks.

HESPERIDAE (SKIPPERS)

Skippers (Hesperiidae) differ fundamentally from other butterflies and may not be closely related at all. Skippers have a short, broad body and broad head with widely separated antennae, and differently positioned wings. The vein pattern of the wings also differs from that of other butterflies.

Approximately forty species are found in Europe but these comprise only a small part of the several thousand species which occur in the world as a whole. Skippers are particularly well represented in the tropics of South America.

The larvae have a large head, live in a tube constructed of leaves bound together by silk and feed mainly on grasses. The larva of one species has been described in no. 250.

195 *Pyrgus malvae*
Grizzled Skipper
Characteristics: Male: Wing length 11–13 mm. Easily recognised by sharply defined white spots on topside of hind wing. Underside of hind wing yellowish- to greenish-brown, with row of white spots across centre often interrupted. Female often larger and ground colour darker brown.
Distribution: Widespread in Europe, as far north as Midlands of British Isles and Scandinavia and Finland north to about 65°N. Eastwards to Pacific coast in Amur region. Subspecies *malvoides* found in southern France, Italy, Spain and Portugal. Common over most of southern England. External characteristics of this subspecies indistinguishable from *malvae malvae*, but genitals differ.
Habitat and Life History: Open terrain, grassy fields, forest clearings, roadsides, up to about 2,000 m. Flight very rapid. Often sits in sun on ground, and at night atop grass or on flowers. In British Isles single generation, on wing May–June, further south two generations, April–June and July–August. Eggs deposited on leaves of wild strawberries (*Fragaria*), cinquefoil (*Potentilla*) and mallow (*Malva*). Larva lives initially under small web, later in rolled leaf. Pupa overwinters.

196 *Pyrgus alveus*
Large Grizzled Skipper
Characteristics: Male and female: Wing length 12–16 mm. Topside of hind wing with very faint light spots, tiny white spots on forewing. Underside of hind wing (no. 196a) olive-brown to greenish with white basal spots, first of which is square.

Has white central band, narrow in cells 2 and 3, clearly defined towards base.
Distribution: Iberian Peninsula and France through southern and central Europe and eastwards through southern Soviet Union to Caucasus and Siberia. Widespread in south-east Norway, central and eastern Sweden and southern Finland.
Habitat and Life History: Central and southern Europe, mainly mountain areas, rarely in lowlands. Lowlands in south-east Sweden, and to 1,200 m in Dovre, Norway. Prefers meadows and slopes rich in flowers; also scattered scrub and barren areas. Single generation on wing July–August. Larva feeds on cinquefoil (*Potentilla*), rock rose (*Helianthemum*) and blackberry (*Rubus*). Eggs overwinter.

197 *Pyrgus armoricanus*
Oberthur's Grizzled Skipper
Characteristics: Male and female: Wing length 12–14 mm. Slightly larger than *malvae* (no. 195), with rather blurred markings on hind wing. Underside similar to no. 196a.
Distribution: Widespread in Europe to southern Scandinavia. Eastwards to Iran, also North Africa.
Habitat and Life History: Dry hills, preferably with scattered scrub. Two generations on wing May–June and July–August. Larva feeds

on leaves of wild strawberries (*Fragaria*) and cinquefoil (*Potentilla*).

198 *Pyrgus serratulae*
Olive Skipper
Characteristics: Male: Wing length 12–14 mm. Topside similar to no. 196, white spots often tiny. Underside of hind wing greenish to olive-green, first white basal spot oval, light central band divided by darker veins. Female has fewer and smaller spots on topside, often with brassy tinge in ground colour.
Distribution: Southern and central Europe north to 52°N, but seldom north of central German mountains, absent from the coastal areas. Mountain areas of Iberian Peninsula and mainland Italy. Eastwards to central Asia.
Habitat and Life History: Mainly mountain meadows up to 2,500 m, rarely in lowlands. Single generation on wing June–August, depending on altitude. Larva feeds on cinquefoil (*Potentilla*).

199 *Pyrgus centaureae*
Northern Grizzled Skipper
Characteristics: Male and female: Wing length 13–15 mm. Topside of forewing with spots similar to *malvae* (no. 195), but without white spot at base of cell 2. Underside of hind wing dark with white veins, dividing dark ground colour into spots.
Distribution: In Europe, Scandin-

avia and Finland north of 60°N. Also northern Soviet Union, Siberia and North America.

Habitat and Life History: Bogs above timber line. Single generation on wing June–July. Larva lives on cloudberry (*Rubus chamaenorus*).

200 *Pyrgus fritillarius*
Safflower Skipper

Characteristics: Male and female: Wing length 15–18 mm. White spot markings on topside well developed, regular row of post-discal spots on hind wing. Underside (no. 200a) has very large, yellowish-grey spots.

Distribution: Southern and central Europe, to Baltic in Poland. Eastwards across southern Soviet Union to central Asia.

Habitat and Life History: Hills, mountains, and dry herbaceous meadows, but everywhere local. Single generation on wing June–September. Usual host plants mallow (*Malva*) and hollyhock (*Althaea*).

201 *Muschampia proto*
Large Grizzled Skipper

Characteristics: Male and female: Wing length 14–15 mm. Distinguished from *Pyrgus* species by absence of white spots in cells 4 and 5 on topside of forewing. Spots along margin obscure and crescent-shaped, variable ground colour of underside of hind wing, with large light central spot and indistinct marginal spots.

Distribution: Iberian Peninsula, south-east France (Provence), Italy, Greece and North Africa, eastwards to Asia Minor.

Habitat and Life History: Uncultivated lowlands and mountains; two to three generations on wing April and throughout summer. Larva lives on *Phlomis*.

202 *Spialia sertorius*
Red-underwing Skipper

Characteristics: Male and female: Wing length 11–14 mm. Topside brownish-black with small white spots, including complete row of marginal spots. Post-discal spots often missing from cells 4 and 5. Underside of hind wing (202a) usually brick red, white spots of central band large, oblong in cells 7 and 8.

Distribution: Southern and central Europe, north to southern Holland and central Germany. Eastwards across western Asia to Tibet and Amur. Also North Africa.

Habitat and Life History: Mountains to 2,000 m and uncultivated lowlands. Two generations on wing April–June and July–August; second generation usually considerably smaller. Larva lives on great burnet (*Sanguisorba*), raspberry (*Rubus idaeus*) and cinquefoil (*Potentilla*).

203 *Carcharodus alceae*
Mallow Skipper

Characteristics: Male and female: Wing length 13–18 mm. Topside dark brown with greyish-brown marbled pattern forming central band and post-discal band on hind wing. Fringes on hind wing chequered. Underside similar to topside, but paler with more distinct spots.

Distribution: Southern and central Europe, north to about 52°N. Eastwards to central Asia. Also North Africa.

Habitat and Life History: Hills and mountains with flower vegetation to 1,500 m. Two generations in lowlands, on wing April–May and July–August; higher up single generation on wing May–June; third generation in very favourable habitats. Larva lives on mallow (*Malva*), and hollyhock (*Althaea*).

204 *Carcharodus lavatherae*
Marbled Skipper
Characteristics: Male and female: Wing length 14–17 mm. Topside of forewing olive-brown, marbled darker with whitish spots. Hind wing darker with clearly-defined white central spots and row of arrow-shaped marginal spots; edge of margin scalloped. Underside of hind wing very light, white with greenish tinge.

Distribution: Southern and central Europe north to 50°N. North Africa and eastwards to Asia Minor.

Habitat and Life History: Local, dry hills and mountain slopes, especially on calcareous soil. Southern European mountains, to

1,800 m. Usually single generation on wing May–August. Larva lives on woundwort (*Stachys*).

205 *Carcharodus boeticus*
Southern Marbled Skipper
Characteristics: Male and female: Wing length 13–16 mm. Topside greyish, marbled darker greyish-brown with lighter spots, hind wing with basal spots, central band and post-discal band. Underside of hind wing yellowish-grey, white veins and rows of spots form reticulate pattern.

Distribution: Portugal, Spain, south-east France, southern alpine valleys, Apennines and Sicily; also North Africa and eastwards to Iran.

Habitat and Life History: Hot localities, in Europe mainly uncultivated places and sunny mountain slopes, from lowlands to 1,500 m. On wing in 2–3 generations May–October. Larva lives in tube spun from leaves of *Marrubium vulgare*, the flowers of which the butterflies visit.

206 *Carcharodus flocciferus*
Tufted Skipper
Characteristics: Male and female: Wing length 14–16 mm. Topside similar to no. 205. Underside (no. 206a) of hind wing greyish-brown with more distinct spots than topside.

Distribution: Southern and central Europe as far north as 40°N.

Habitat and Life History: Same as no. 205.

207 *Erynnis tages*
Dingy Skipper
Characteristics: Male and female: Wing length 13–14 mm. Topside dark brown, row of small, pale marginal spots on both wings, two powdery grey bands on forewing. Underside paler brown, with only small, light marginal spots similar to topside.
Distribution: Widely distributed in Europe; in Sweden and Norway as far north as 62°N. Very common in south of British Isles, rare in Scotland, isolated colonies in Ireland. East through Soviet Union and Siberia to China.
Habitat and Life History: Open terrain, roadsides, along edges woods, heaths, forest meadows. In mountains up to 1,800 m. Likes to sit with unfolded wings in sun on bare ground, but difficult to see in flight. In overcast weather and at night, sits head downwards under dry flower heads. Single generation on wing May–June. Eggs deposited singly on birdsfoot trefoil (*Lotus corniculatus*) and other members of pea family. For larva: see no. 250.

208 *Heteropterus morpheus*
Large Chequered Skipper
Characteristics: Male and female: Wing length 16–18 mm. Topside brownish-black with 3–4 light spots near costa on forewing.

Underside (no. 208a) of forewing brownish-black with yellow apical markings. Underside of hind wing with twelve whitish black-ringed 'mirror-spots', black marginal line, and black edge along inner margin.
Distribution: Northern Spain, western France, southern Switzerland, northern Italy, Holland, northern Germany, through eastern Europe. Eastwards through Soviet Union and central Asia to Amur region and Korea.
Habitat and Life History: Damp meadows with abundant flowers, forest clearings, along forest roads; lowlands only. Single generation on wing from late June to early August. Larva lives on various large grasses, making closely-spun tube of grass in which it overwinters. During following spring, larva lives more freely on food plants. Pupates upon grass leaf.

209 *Carterocephalus palaemon*
Chequered Skipper
Characteristics: Male and female: Wing length 13–14 mm. Topside dark brown with large yellow-brown basal and post-discal spots and with small marginal spots on forewing; single basal spot, two central and row of small post-discal spots of same colour on hind wing. Ground colour of underside paler grey-brown with similar markings.
Distribution: North-west France through central and eastern

Europe and Balkans. Southern limit in Pyrenees. Found rarely in small area of Midlands of British Isles. South-west Norway and northern Sweden to arctic circle, most of Finland.

Habitat and Life History: Rare and local in Europe. Lowland species, found in forest bogs and meadows, along roads and streams. Single generation on wing June and July. Has short, quick flight; sits with unfolded wings in sun. Larva lives on various grasses, overwinters, but does not eat after hibernation.

210 *Carterocephalus silvicolus*
Northern Chequered Skipper

Characteristics: Male: Wing length 12–14 mm. Topside of forewing pale yellow with large, black central spots and small, black marginal spots. Underside similar. Dark areas more widespread on female.

Distribution: North-eastern Europe eastwards to Japan. Also North America.

Habitat and Life History: Frequents open, warm, damp woods and hills, preferably rich with flowers. Single generation on wing June–July. Larva feeds on grasses.

211 *Thymelicus acteon*
Lulworth Skipper

Characteristics: Male: Wing length 11–13 mm. Topside yellowish-brown, often with thick grey

dust, and light stripe in central cell; curved row of small yellowish spots in post-discal area of forewing. Underside plain yellowish-brown. Male has distinct spot of scent scales from vein 1 to vein 3. Female (no. 211a) similar to male, often with darker dust.

Distribution: Local in southern and central Europe to about 48°N. In British Isles, isolated colonies on Dorset and Devon coast. North Africa and eastwards to Asia Minor and Middle East.

Habitat and Life History: Meadows and dry, grassy hills and mountain slopes. Single generation on wing May to late August. Larva feeds on grasses.

212 *Thymelicus lineola*
Essex Skipper

Characteristics: Male and female: Wing length 12–14 mm. Topside almost plain golden-brown with darker marginal border. Male has inconspicuous stripe of scent scales parallel to vein 2. Tip of antenna black (cf. no. 213). Underside of hind wing plain yellowish-brown to yellowish-grey.

Distribution: Widespread in Europe north to 62°N, in Scandinavia and Finland. In British Isles, Cambridgeshire, Suffolk and Somerset. Soviet Union and central Asia to Amur region. Also North Africa.

Habitat and Life History: Grassland with flowers. Flies quickly from flower to flower. Single generation

on wing July–August. Female
deposits eggs on grasses. Larva
does not hatch until following
April, fully grown in two months.

213 *Thymelicus sylvestris*
Small Skipper
Characteristics: Male and female:
Wing length 13–15 mm. Similar
to previous species, but male's
stripe of scent scales more distinct,
longer, more curved and crosses
veins. Tip of antenna yellowish-
brown underneath. Underside of
hind wing with fairly defined
reddish area.
Distribution: Southern and central
Europe to southern coast of
Baltic. Locally common in southern counties and Midlands of
British Isles, less common in
Wales, rare in Scotland. Eastwards to Asia Minor and Iran.
Also North Africa.
Habitat and Life History: Similar to
no. 212.

214 *Ochlodes venatus*
Large Skipper
Characteristics: Male: Wing length
14–17 mm. Topside yellowish-
brown, darker along margin with
distinct black stripe of scent
scales. Underside of hind wing
golden-brown with faint yellow
spots. Female darker near base
and in centre. Topside of hind
wing dark brown with row of paler
central spots.
Distribution: Widely distributed
in Europe, northern limit about

63°N. In British Isles, not in
Scotland or Ireland. Also absent
from southern Spain. Eastwards
through temperate areas of Asia
to China and Japan.
Habitat and Life History: Grassy
forest edges, and near coasts.
Single generation on wing June–
August. Flies restlessly from flower
to flower. Larva feeds on grasses.

215 *Hesperia comma*
Silver-spotted Skipper
Characteristics: Male and female:
Wing length 14–15 mm. Topside
very similar to no. 214, but
stripe of scent scales very cons-
picuous and ridged, includes some
bluish-grey scales; corner of hind
wing pronounced, but rounded.
Underside of hind wing (no. 215a)
olive-green with white spots. Female more clearly marked than
male.
Distribution: Widely distributed in
Europe, but only in south-east of
British Isles. Eastwards across
temperate areas of Asia. Also
western North America.
Habitat and Life History: Mainly
dry grass fields; often on calcareous
soil. Single generation on wing
July–August. Larva feeds on
grasses such as sheep fescue
(*Festuca ovina*) and hair grass
(*Aira*) species. Hatches in spring
after egg has overwintered.

216 *Gegenes nostrodamus*
Mediterranean Skipper
Characteristics: Male: Wing length

15–16 mm. Topside plain greyish-brown. Underside similar to topside, hind wing paler towards inner margin. Female has several white spots on forewing on both top- and underside, largest towards back.

Distribution: Spain, Italy, Balkans and North Africa. Eastwards through Asia Minor and Middle East to India.

Habitat and Life History: European populations favour warm gorges and dry river-beds near coast. Two generations on wing April–June and August–September; second brood more numerous. Larva lives on grasses.

BUTTERFLY LARVAE AND PUPAE

217 *Parnassius apollo*
Apollo
Larva hatches in early spring, often when snow still on ground. Eats leaves of stonecrop (*Sedum*), but only when sunny. Larva fully grown in June, about 50 mm long. Like papilionid larvae, has fork-shaped projection on neck. Larva spins loose cocoon on ground, often hidden under stone; 8–10 days later butterfly emerges. For butterfly: see no. 1.

218 *Papilio machaon*
Swallowtail
Larva hatches from the egg in 8–10 days. At first black, with or without red spots, with black spines and big white spot on back. Larva fully grown in a month, 40–50 mm long, with colours as illustrated. Behind head is fork-shaped reddish-yellow organ which larva everts when threatened. Organ produces pungent smell resembling odour of orange peel. Whereas young larva is well camouflaged (looks like a bird's dropping), fully grown larva has warning colours. Eats during day, especially umbels of host plants. Pupa 30 mm long, colour variable, suspended on tree trunk, stalk, or similar by two hooks on tip of abdomen. Pupa of first generation produces minor second brood in late summer or over-winters until following spring. For butterfly: see no. 6.

219 *Aporia crataegi*
Black-veined White
Larvae live socially in common web until pupation in following year. In October web divides, larvae winter in separate webs until April, when they resume feeding for short time. When 9 months old larvae are 35–40 mm long. When abundant can damage fruit trees. Pupa (no. 219a), sus-

pended in host tree, is very similar to pupa no. 220. Pupation about 3 weeks. For butterfly: see no. 10.

220 *Pieris brassicae*
Large White
Larvae live socially on wild and cultivated crucifers, especially cabbage (*Brassica*). Development takes about a month. Fully grown larva 40 mm long, greyish-green with three yellow longitudinal stripes, whole body covered with black warts and spots. Larva often infested with parasitic wasps. Sulphur-yellow cocoons of wasp *Apanteles glomeratus* form ring around dead larva. Usually pupates on walls, poles; takes about 2 weeks in summer, while pupal stage of hibernating brood lasts about 8 months. Green or ivory pupa is angular with black stripes and spots. For butterfly: see no. 11.

221 *Pieris rapae*
Small White
Larva hatches in 3–7 days. Fully grown in 3 weeks, and about 25 mm long. Similar to no. 220. Larva of spring generation usually pupates on host plant, whereas larva of summer generation pupates on walls. Over 90 per cent of pupae may be infested with parasites. For butterfly: see no. 12.

222 *Anthoharis cardamines*
Orange Tip
Slim, bluish-green larva, mainly eats fruits of crucifers. Fully grown

larva about 30 mm long. Larva leaves host plant to find more solid stems and branches in which to pupate. Colour of pupa (no. 222a) variable. Pupates 10–11 months before butterfly (see no. 21) emerges following spring.

223 *Colias palaeno*
Moorland Clouded Yellow
Larva overwinters. In spring eats leaves of bog whortleberry (*Vaccinium uliginosum*). Fully grown May–June, 30–35 mm long, green with prominent yellow side stripe and white black-ringed stigmata. Yellowish-green pupa has curved back. For butterfly, which appears month later, see no. 25.

224 *Gonepteryx rhamni*
Brimstone
Larva hatches soon after egg laid April–May; fully grown, about 30 mm long, in 4 weeks; dull green, darkest on head. Pupa (no. 224a) usually found on underside of leaf. Butterfly (see no. 30) appears approximately 2 weeks later, on wing until autumn frosts force it to hibernate.

225 *Apatura iris*
Purple Emperor
Larva hatches in about 2 weeks, at first living in a small web on tip of willow leaf. At night emerges from web to eat edge of leaf. Half-grown larva overwinters attached to branch. Larva resumes

eating when fresh leaves appear in following spring; fully grown larva 40–50 mm long, characteristically slug-like, green with yellow diagonal stripes, head bluish-green with two horns forming V. Pupates on leaf; pupa attached by small hooks to a silk pad on underside of leaf. For butterfly: see no. 34.

226 *Limenitis camilla*
White Admiral
In September young larva spins tube between leaves where it overwinters; in spring resumes feeding until fully grown in May–June. 30–40 mm long, yellowish-green with reddish-brown ventral side, with long back spines bearing bristly brushes on segments 2, 3, 5, 10 and 11. Larval stage lasts about 10 months. Pupa attached by hind end to small cocoon on twig or leaf stalk, pale green or greyish-white with metallic spots, with two projections on head resembling ears, large hump on thorax. Butterfly (no. 39) emerges 2 weeks after pupation.

227 *Nymphalis antiopa*
Camberwell Beauty
In spring young larvae live socially in web on birch (*Betula*) and willow (*Salix*). From web eat leaves until fourth casting of skin at about 6 weeks. Fully grown larva 50–55 mm long, black with rust-red back spots and prominent black back spines.

Pupa is suspended, brownish-grey without metallic spots, with pointed head. Butterfly (no. 41) hibernates.

228 *Inachis io*
Peacock
In spring larvae live socially on common nettle (*Urtica dioica*). Fully grown larva 40 mm long, black with white spots and long black dorsal spines. Most larvae pupate suspended on tree trunks. Pupa greyish-brown or greenish with metallic gold spots. Pupates in 2 weeks, butterfly (no. 44) overwinters.

229 *Vanessa atalanta*
Red Admiral
Larva feeds on common nettle (*Urtica dioica*), from which it spins pocket. Fully grown larva 30 mm long, with variable colour: velvety black, greenish-brown or reddish, with seven rows of spines. Pupa suspended in cocoon on underside of leaf. Butterfly (no. 46) emerges in 2–3 weeks.

230 *Aglais urticae*
Small Tortoiseshell
Larvae live socially in large web on common nettle (*Urtica dioica*). When leaves consumed, larvae move to another plant. Larva fully grown in 4 weeks, 20 mm long, brownish-black with yellowish back, side stripes with black-tipped yellow spines. Does not pupate on host plant. Pupa,

greyish-brown, often with metallic spots, is suspended from posts, walls, sheds and tree trunks. For butterfly: see no. 48.

231 *Araschnia levana*
Map Butterfly
Larvae live socially on common nettle (*Urtica dioica*). Fully grown larva black and yellowish-brown with black stripes and yellowish or black branched spines. Pupa brown with darker wing sheaths and spots; head has two points and metallic spots. Pupae of summer generation overwinter. For butterfly: see no. 51.

232 *Argynnis paphia*
Silver-washed Fritillary
Larva overwinters in cracks in bark of oaks (*Quercus*) and firs (*Pinus*). In spring, larva crawls down to forest floor to eat leaves of violets (*Viola*). Fully grown in 6–7 weeks, about 40 mm long, purple-brown to black with pale yellow dorsal stripe and dark yellow spines. Pupa resembles rolled-up dead leaf and is suspended under branches. For butterfly: see no. 49.

233 *Mesoacidalia aglaja*
Dark-green Fritillary
Larva overwinters on violets (*Viola*) without eating, but eats the fresh violets in spring. Measures 35 mm when fully grown. Black with double white dorsal line, with six rows of black spines, also red side spots. Pupates in June; butterfly (see no. 52) emerges 4 weeks later.

234 *Fabriciana niobe*
Niobe Fritillary
Eggs overwinter on moss, larva hatching in spring. Larva eats violet (*Viola*) species. Measures 40 mm long. Brown with yellowish-brown ventral side, white dorsal line edged with black, triangular white spot on side of each segment; dorsal spines pale red. Larva pupates May–June. For butterfly: see no. 54.

235 *Brenthis ino*
Lesser Marbled Fritillary
Larva eats in autumn and the following spring after hibernation. Active only during night. Fully grown larva about 35 mm, yellowish-grey with darker brown back stripe with light edges, yellowish side stripe and yellow spines. Pupa yellowish-brown, marbled dark with yellow dorsal spines. For butterfly: see no. 58.

236 *Mellicta athalia*
Heath Fritillary
In autumn larvae live socially and overwinter in web. After hibernation they separate and live singly until pupation in May. Fully grown larva about 25 mm long. Pupa, suspended by abdominal spines, is whitish-grey with black markings and small reddish-

yellow buds on topside of abdomen. Butterfly (see no. 75) emerges 2 weeks later.

237 *Euphydryas maturna*
Scarce Fritillary
Larvae live in colony in web surrounding leaves, especially ash (*Fraxinus*). In autumn web falls to ground with leaves, and larvae overwinter in it. Next spring, the larvae live singly on low-growing plants. Pupate on stones and tree trunks. For butterfly: see no. 79.

238 *Melanargia galathea*
Marbled White
Larva overwinters on grass before eating. Feeds on grasses in early spring. Pupation May–June on ground among grass and moss. For butterfly: see no. 83.

239 *Hipparchia semele*
Grayling
Larva overwinters after second moult. After winter, eats grass. About 30 mm long when fully grown. Active only at night; during day hides among dead leaves. Pupates in June. Larva burrows 10–12 mm into sandy soil, lining cavity with web. Pupates in chamber after about 1 month. For butterfly: see no. 91.

240 *Erebia medusa*
Woodland Ringlet
Larva lives on millet grass (*Milium*), development taking 2 years. Fully grown larva 20 mm long, greenish or brownish with a black dorsal band, lighter side stripes and dark foot stripes. Pupa overwinters on ground. For butterfly: see no. 108.

241 *Maniola jurtina*
Meadow Brown
Larva hatches in early autumn. Moults 5 times and overwinters before reaching maximum length of about 25 mm. During day larva hides among grass roots, eating only at night. Larva greenish with lighter side stripes, whole body closely covered with small, dark spots. Pupa suspended from food plant, is greenish with yellow and brown spots. Pupation takes 4 weeks. For butterfly: see no. 120.

242 *Coenonympha pamphilus*
Small Heath
Larva lives on grasses, overwintering after third moult, but may eat during mild winter. Mainly feeds at night. Fully grown about 20 mm long, yellowish-green with darker green underside and three dark green dorsal stripes and broad side stripe. Two reddish and white projections with short white spines on tip of abdomen. Larvae of summer generation pupate after 1 month. Pupa short and stout, 8–9 mm long, light with dark green spots and two rows of white warts on sides of abdomen. Pupates in about a month. For butterfly: see no. 127.

243 *Lasiommata megera*
Wall Brown

Larva lives on grasses. Fully grown, 30 mm long, before winter. Green with dark green dorsal stripe and three lighter side stripes. Whole body slightly downy. Pupa suspended by abdomen. Pupal stage of summer generation about 2 weeks, but pupal stage of hibernating generation 6–7 months. Fully grown larva also overwinters. For butterfly: see no. 134.

244 *Thecla betulae*
Brown Hairstreak

Larva hatches in spring. For 6 weeks, larva eats fresh leaves of sloe and other *Prunus* species. By June fully grown, about 18 mm long. Bluish-green with yellow dorsal and side stripes, yellow oblique stripes and brown head. Larva is broad and flat and difficult to see on leaf. Before pupation larva turns reddishviolet. Pupa smooth, round and pale brown. Pupation 3–4 weeks. For butterfly: see no. 139.

245 *Callophrys rubi*
Green Hairstreak

Larva feeds on various plants and is also cannibalistic. Larva fully grown in 3–4 weeks, 15 mm long, green with yellow markings and short, brown, prickly hairs. Pupates in loose web under plants and overwinters. Has a characteristic squeak. For butterfly: see no. 148.

246 *Lycaena phlaeas*
Small Copper

Larva at first lives in grooves it makes on surface of leaf of sorrel (*Rumex*) species. Later gnaws through leaf. Larva shaped like woodlouse, dark green, often with reddish markings, covered with short, reddish-brown bristles. Hibernating larva rests on silk web on underside of leaves. Pupa ochre-brown with black spots, attached to leaf or stalk. Pupation about 1 month. For butterfly: see no. 151.

247 *Heodes virgaureae*
Scarce Copper

Larva hatches from overwintered eggs in April, living mainly on *Rumex* species, such as common sorrel. Fully grown in June, 20 mm long. Green with yellowish-green dorsal and side stripes, yellow dorsally. Pupation takes 1 month in June. For butterfly: see no. 154.

248 *Cupido minimus*
Small Blue

At first larva lives in flower of kidney vetch (*Anthyllis*). After second moult larva may be cannibalistic. After third moult larva is fully grown, approximately 10 mm long, usually yellowish-green with red stripes dorsally. Larva overwinters in dead flowers when difficult to see. Larval stage lasts approximately 11 months. Pupa attached to grass with head upwards. Pupation about 2 weeks. For butterfly: see no. 164.

249 *Lysandra bellargus*
Adonis Blue
Larva lives on various plants of pea family and overwinters. Fully grown larva about 18 mm long, greenish or pale brown with dark dorsal stripes and reddish-yellow triangular spots on sides. Larva active at night and visited by various ants which milk it for sweet secretion from glands.

Pupates on plant. For butterfly: see no. 193.

250 *Erynnis tages*
Dingy Skipper
Larva lives between two leaves spun together and eats their surfaces. Larva fully grown after often 4–5 weeks and four moults, is 18 mm long. Its head is dark and much larger than first segment of thorax, generally green with many spines. Pupates in April after overwintering. For butterfly: see no. 207.

BIBLIOGRAPHY

A few more titles to supplement the information in this book:

Dickens, M. and Storey, E., *The World of Butterflies*, Osprey, 1972.
Ford, E. B., *Butterflies*, Collins, 1971.
Higgins, L. G. and Riley, N. D., *A Field Guide to the Butterflies of Britain*, Collins, 1973.
Howarth, T. G., *Colour Identification Guides to British Butterflies*, Warne, 1973.
Mansell, F. and Newman, L. Hugh, *The Complete British Butterflies in Colour*, Michael Joseph, 1968.

INDEX OF LATIN NAMES

The figures refer to the illustration and description numbers

INDEX OF ENGLISH NAMES

The figures refer to the illustration and description numbers